Productive
Group Work

ASCD MEMBER BOOK

Many ASCD members received this book as a
member benefit upon its initial release.

Learn more at: **www.ascd.org/memberbooks**

Productive
Group Work

How to Engage Students, Build Teamwork, and Promote Understanding

Nancy Frey · Douglas Fisher · Sandi Everlove

Alexandria, Virginia USA

1703 N. Beauregard St. • Alexandria, VA 22311-1714 USA
Phone: 800-933-2723 or 703-578-9600 • Fax: 703-575-5400
Web site: www.ascd.org • E-mail: member@ascd.org
Author guidelines: www.ascd.org/write

Gene R. Carter, *Executive Director;* Nancy Modrak, *Publisher;* Scott Willis, *Director, Book Acquisitions & Development;* Julie Houtz, *Director, Book Editing & Production;* Katie Martin, *Editor;* Catherine Guyer, *Senior Graphic Designer;* Mike Kalyan, *Production Manager;* Circle Graphics, *Typesetter;* Kyle Steichen, *Production Specialist*

All Web links in this book are correct as of the publication date below but may have become inactive or otherwise modified since that time. If you notice a deactivated or changed link, please e-mail books@ascd.org with the words "Link Update" in the subject line. In your message, please specify the Web link, the book title, and the page number on which the link appears.

ASCD Member Book, No. FY10-02 (Nov. 2009, PSI+). ASCD Member Books mail to Premium (P), Select (S), and Institutional Plus (I+) members on this schedule: Jan., PSI+; Feb., P; Apr., PSI+; May, P; July, PSI+; Aug., P; Sept., PSI+; Nov., PSI+; Dec., P. Select membership was formerly known as Comprehensive membership.

PAPERBACK ISBN: 978-1-4166-0883-7   ASCD product #109018
Also available as an e-book (see Books in Print for the ISBNs).

Quantity discounts for the paperback edition only: 10–49 copies, 10%; 50+ copies, 15%; for 1,000 or more copies, call 800-933-2723, ext. 5634, or 703-575-5634. For desk copies: member@ascd.org.

Library of Congress Cataloging-in-Publication Data

Frey, Nancy, 1959–
   Productive group work : how to engage students, build teamwork, and promote understanding / Nancy Frey, Douglas Fisher, and Sandi Everlove.
      p. cm.
   Includes bibliographical references and index.
   ISBN 978-1-4166-0883-7 (pbk. : alk. paper) 1. Group work in education. 2. Team learning approach in education. 3. Active learning. I. Fisher, Douglas. II. Everlove, Sandi. III. Title.
   LB1032.F78 2009
   371.3'6—dc22
                                                                                      2009028551

20 19 18 17 16 15 14 13 12 11 10 09   1 2 3 4 5 6 7 8 9 10 11 12

Productive
Group Work

How to Engage Students, Build Teamwork, and Promote Understanding

Acknowledgments

We were encouraged in this project by Dr. Robert Hill of the Ball Foundation, which partners with midsize urban schools to increase student literacy. The foundation's work with partner district Northview Schools in Grand Rapids, Michigan, provided many of this book's classroom examples of productive group work. We thank the foundation and Northview teachers, administrators, and program staff for their generosity in sharing their classrooms and experiences with us and for their encouragement and friendship.

Doug and Nancy would also like to thank their coauthor, Sandi, for providing the impetus for this book and for sharing her experiences with productive group work acquired through her classroom teaching and travels with TeachFirst.

Introduction

Groups are smart. From the earliest interest in how groups work at the beginning of the 20th century to research today, evidence gathered has shown that "under the right circumstances, groups are remarkably intelligent, and are often smarter than the smartest people in them" (Surowiecki, 2005, p. xiii). We are not suggesting that teachers turn their classrooms over to student collaboration in the absence of instruction, but we *are* suggesting that productive group work be considered a necessary part of good teaching.

The key to getting the most out of group work, to having groups be truly productive, is creating those "right circumstances." In this book, we hope to show you what those favorable conditions are and how to produce them in your classroom. When teachers get the circumstances right, something remarkable happens: Students educate one another and end up knowing more than they would have working alone.

What does productive group work look like? You might see it, as we did, in Amber Johnson's social science class, where students were studying American Indians and their food supplies. One of the productive group tasks involved researching food sources. Each group was assigned a different food source, and every member of the group had to locate information to share with their groupmates. Students had access to the Internet and a collection of books. Their task was to summarize their findings in writing as a group, with each member of the group contributing at least one sentence (written in a different color ink). In addition, each group member had to be able to explain the contents of the entire paper to the teacher during her interviews with students. A paragraph from the paper of the group assigned to acorns follows (font changes represent different students' writing):

> Collecting acorns is a complicated task; you'll need to be able to identify the good from the bad. When you look for acorns in the fall, when they are ripe, they may fall to the ground. When you start to collect them, be sure to collect the ones with their "caps," for if you do collect the capless ones, they may have insect larvae inside. This is mainly because an acorn without a cap has likely fallen, due to the worm's activity in the acorn, causing it to shake loose of the cap. You must also heavily scrutinize the ones you did manage to collect for holes in the acorns' shell, as these will also indicate the presence of a foul acorn.

The paragraph makes sense and conveys accurate and interesting information. More importantly, it represents the collaborative knowledge of a group of students working together and sharing information. This opportunity to consolidate knowledge with peers also prepares students for completing later independent tasks, readying them for the eventuality of independent learning.

All of us gain knowledge through peer interaction. It's part of daily life. A few years ago, while attending an education conference, we noted just such an instance of informal group learning. It didn't take place during a conference session, but as a group of us were having breakfast.

That morning, we woke up to news that a man named John Mark Karr had confessed to being involved in the murder of JonBenét Ramsey. He had been arrested and was being flown from Thailand to Colorado. Each of us read the newspaper article, and, being teachers, we applied the kinds of comprehension strategies that we routinely teach. It wasn't hard for any of us to identify the article's main idea, locate supporting facts, visualize, summarize, infer, and the like. But it was not this article's content that stands out in our memory, but the group conversation it led to.

Our breakfast table that morning was abuzz with conversation. Finally, it seemed, the killer had been found, and the Ramsey family could get closure. Then, one of the members of the group expressed frustration: "Why did the criminal get to fly first class? I came here in coach!" The conversation changed direction as we talked about this. At one point, another member of the breakfast group asked, "So, is our recommendation that he should have traveled in coach, where there are more children?" We decided that putting the suspect in first class had probably been a good idea, if only to keep other travelers safe. Someone else wondered, "But why did he get to drink—champagne, was it?—during the flight?"

This question triggered a number of perspectives, experiences, and reactions. The conversation turned from the newspaper article to the legal system. Could evidence obtained under the influence of alcohol while in police custody be used in court? None of us was sure about this, but we all wanted to know. The group work, our face-to-face interaction with information, provoked interest and inquiry. It required that we present information from the text and explain nuances. We had to infer. We had to listen, debate, and negotiate. And as a result, we validated and extended our own understanding. We learned from one another.

Educators have understood the importance of collaborative group learning for decades. A large body of research shows that students involved in cooperative work demonstrate higher levels of academic learning and retention than their peers working individually. This increase in learning has been seen in elementary, middle, and high school students across disciplines. For example, in a comparison study, 2nd grade students in classrooms that stressed cooperative learning were found to perform better on a measure of reading comprehension than those in traditional classrooms (Law, 2008). A large-scale analysis derived from the Third International Mathematics and Science Study (TIMSS) of almost 5,000 Japanese 13-year-old science students found that the use of small-group cooperative learning activities was positively associated with science achievement scores (House, 2005). Similar results were obtained in a meta-analysis of studies on the effects of cooperative learning on high school and undergraduate chemistry students (Bowen, 2000).

Equally impressive is that cooperative group work has been shown to result in increased self-esteem, improved relationships among students, and enhanced social and education skills. Studies have demonstrated group work's positive effects on inter-actions among students in middle school (Gillies, 2008), and middle school students also reported that they favored this type of learning over working independently (Mueller & Fleming, 2001). Elementary students in classrooms that used cooperative learning techniques were found to have higher levels of motivation and a more positive perception of school (Battistich, Solomon, & Delucchi, 1993).

Group Work Gone Wrong

Although the effectiveness of collaborative learning is well documented, we are also acutely aware of its failures. They are the reason so many students resist working in groups and why some teachers avoid using group work in their classrooms.

Most students (and many teachers) have never experienced genuine collaborative learning. For a majority of us, our experience of academic group work consists of being thrown together into a group and then expected to create a product, learn a skill, or accomplish a task without additional support from the instructor. The group frequently starts out with good intentions but often ends with one or two students taking over and doing the lion's share of the work while the rest play minor roles. The "worker bees" often feel put upon, taken advantage of, or shackled by their peers, while sidelined members of the group frequently feel inadequate, unable to keep up, or that they have nothing valuable to contribute. Whether students experience group work as a worker bee, gopher, or hitchhiker, the end results are generally the same—lots of frustration and too little real learning.

Doug remembers having just such an experience as a high school student in a large public school that was attempting to implement cooperative learning. Unfortunately, the tasks his teachers assigned did not require individual accountability. Instead, groups of students worked together to produce one "thing." For example, his government teacher assigned research topics to groups of students and gave each group a pile of forms to fill out in preparation for a group paper and group speech. One of these forms required that the group summarize the positive and negative aspects of their assigned topic. (The topic assigned to Doug's group was laetrile as a cancer treatment.) Their assignment was to address specific areas of concern, including economic, government/freedom, health, safety, moral/justice, religious, legal, and aesthetic.

Doug understood early on in his high school career that it was beneficial to choose group partners who wanted to work hard and please the teacher; the harder the other members of his group were willing to work, the less he had to. In other words, Doug was a hitchhiker, and, as a result, he did very little work in high school. (College, he notes, was a shock, and he had to struggle to develop good study habits and time management skills.)

For this particular project in government class, Doug's group completed and submitted, on time, each and every form provided—all 18 of them. The group got an *A* on the packet, an *A* on the essay, and an *A* on the speech. Doug recalls being part of the group but not doing any of the prep work or essay writing. He does remember giving part of the speech, which was written by another member of the group. Obviously, Doug did not get very much out of this experience, and neither, he imagines, did his teacher, who would have been unable to determine which students understood the content and which did not. Here, the failed implementation of cooperative learning groups resulted in failure to check for understanding or link instruction with performance. Because the group work had not been designed to yield information about individual student performance, the teacher was left to assume that every member of the group understood the content equally well.

Although Doug's teacher may not have recognized that these collaborative learning efforts were unsuccessful, most teachers *do* know when group work has gone awry. Mathematics teacher Grace Coates described an early, unsatisfying foray into group learning this way:

> Where I had imagined cooperative dialogue, there was bickering and arguing over materials. Where I had envisioned smiles, many students wore sullen looks. A few wore triumphant smiles as they managed to take over the work or materials. Where I had hoped for thoughtful curiosity, there were pleading looks saying, "What do I do?" I was so disappointed by these results and my inability to change things in a way that would get my students working productively. (2005, p. 11)

While Coates originally believed that the grouping alone would take care of everything, she came to realize that her students needed to learn how to communicate with one another over a meaningful task.

Because group work is so much a part of adult daily life, we can easily underestimate the thinking, planning, and skill development necessary for our students to work together successfully. Teachers know group work is beneficial, but they start out without having identified and established the right conditions. Education specialist Elizabeth Cohen (1994) notes that "the teacher who has no more tools for the planning of group work than an initial attraction to an idea . . . is likely to run into trouble" (p. 22).

In writing this book, our goal is to give you, a classroom teacher, the tools and knowledge you need to design and guide group work that is successful—that is productive. As you will see in Chapter 1, our approach expands on prior cooperative learning research (e.g., Johnson & Johnson, 1994) and includes newer information about backward planning and differentiated instruction. In the kind of *productive group work* you will be reading about in the pages to come, all students are engaged with the academic content and with each other, and the end result is consolidated and extended knowledge for all.

Productive Group Work in the Bigger Instructional Picture

This book is also a natural next step in support of the gradual release of responsibility model of instruction, the focus of Doug and Nancy's book *Better Learning Through Structured Teaching* (Fisher & Frey, 2008a). The gradual release of responsibility model stipulates that the teacher move from assuming "all the responsibility for performing a task . . . to a situation in which the students assume all of the responsibility" (Duke & Pearson, 2002, p. 211). This gradual release may occur over a day, a week, a month, or a year. The teacher begins by modeling the desired learning. Over time, students assume more responsibility for the task, moving from being participants in the modeled lesson, to apprentices in shared instruction, to collaborators with their peers, and finally, to independent performers (see Figure A).

The framework's components are as follows:

1. *Focus lesson:* The teacher establishes the lesson's purpose and models his or her own thinking for students to illustrate how to approach the new learning.

2. *Guided instruction:* The teacher strategically uses assessment-informed prompts, cues, and questions to guide students to increasingly complex thinking and facilitate students' increased responsibility for task completion.

3. *Collaborative learning:* The teacher designs and supervises tasks that enable students to consolidate their thinking and understanding—and that require students to generate individual products that can provide formative assessment information.

4. *Independent tasks:* The teacher designs and supervises tasks that require students to apply information they have been taught to create new and authentic

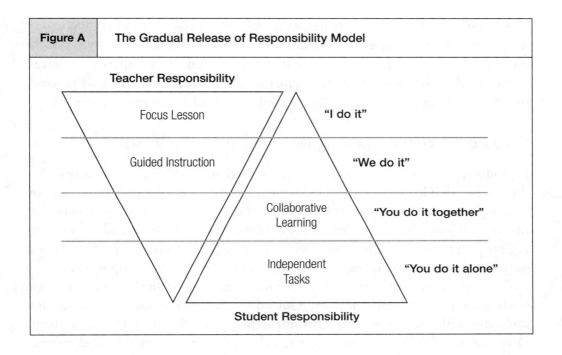

| Figure A | The Gradual Release of Responsibility Model |

Teacher Responsibility

Focus Lesson — "I do it"

Guided Instruction — "We do it"

Collaborative Learning — "You do it together"

Independent Tasks — "You do it alone"

Student Responsibility

products. This phase of the instructional framework is ideal for the "spiral review" that so many educators know their students need, and it is a way to build students' confidence by allowing them to demonstrate their expanding competence.

Our focus on productive group work is an attempt to rectify the fact that many current implementations of the gradual release of responsibility model focus primarily on teacher/student interactions and overlook student/student interactions: learning through collaboration with peers. Productive group work provides students an opportunity to collaborate to complete specific tasks. Sometimes the teacher develops and guides these tasks, and other times the tasks are student initiated and student led. Regardless, these tasks provide students an opportunity to work together to solve problems, discover information, and complete projects.

The best productive group work tasks allow students to apply what they have learned during teacher-modeled focus lessons and guided instruction, and they prepare students for independent learning, which is the ultimate goal of instruction. Less-effective tasks are those that are disconnected from the course of study or topic. Too often, these less-than-effective tasks have been the mainstay of group work, which is why we believe teachers too rarely employ the collaboration component of the gradual release of responsibility model. In this book, you will meet several teachers who buck this trend and, instead, regularly use productive group work as part of a gradual release of responsibility to ensure that all students learn. Before we proceed, though, it's worth pausing to consider the role of the teacher during group work.

Guiding Instruction During Productive Group Work

If productive group work is primarily about student collaboration, what is it that the teacher should be doing? Nancy remembers supervising group work tasks by walking around the classroom. At the risk of dating herself, she likens herself at that time to Julie, the cruise director on *The Love Boat*. Her job seemed to be checking on people to see if they were OK and having fun. Since those days, she has learned a great deal about the teacher's role during productive group work.

We have introduced the idea of guided instruction and defined it as the strategic use of cues, prompts, and questions. Guided instruction is a teacher behavior that can occur with the whole class, with small groups, or with an individual student. Determining when to use whole-class, small-group, or individual guided instruction is something teachers often have to decide by observing students as a lesson unfolds. For example, after establishing the purpose of a lesson by explaining that they will work on analyzing data for probabilities, Ms. Anderson might model how to solve a probability problem as follows:

> A spinner has four equal sectors colored yellow, blue, green, and red. What are the chances of landing on blue after spinning the spinner? What are the chances of landing on red?

Next, she shares her thinking about this problem:

> I see that there are four color choices. Each color on the spinner seems to take up the same amount of space, and the question says that the four sectors are equal. I know that this means that I have the same chance of landing on red as blue or green or yellow. I also know that the spinner has to stop on only one color. So, thinking about the first question, I know that there is only one way to land on blue and that is if the spinner stops there. So I'll put the number one on the top or as the numerator. For the denominator, I have to think about all of the

possibilities. There are four colors, so the spinner could land on any of the four. Four is my denominator. Therefore, my ratio is 1/4. So, I have a one-fourth, or 25-percent chance, of landing on blue.

Following this modeling, Ms. Anderson introduces the next problem:

What is the probability of choosing a vowel from the alphabet?

For this problem, she uses whole-class guided instruction. She starts with questions:

Ms. Anderson: What do I need to know to start thinking about this problem?

Martha: How many vowels there are.

Ms. Anderson: Excellent, yes. And how many vowels are there in English, Edgar?

Edgar: Five or six, depending on if you count y.

Ms. Anderson: Good point. For this problem, let's agree to use the five common vowels. Now, what else do we need to know to solve this problem?

Coriama: The denominator. It's 26, because English has a total of 26 letters.

Ms. Anderson: Yes, exactly. So which number is the numerator, and which is the denominator? Write your ideas on your dry-erase boards and hold them up for me.

At this point, Ms. Anderson scans the room waiting for her students to write "5/26" on their boards and show her. Most of her students have the correct answer, but four do not. She concludes that the majority of the class is ready for productive group work related to probability, and four students need additional guided instruction. Ms. Anderson knows that the students who understood the problem do not need additional guided instruction. She invites them to work on a problem set in their previously established math triads, giving them this instruction:

Remember to solve each problem in three ways: with numbers; with words; and with a model, illustration, or image. You'll need to talk about your answers with one another using your approach. If you were the number person on problem 1, then you're the word person on problem 2, and so on. You'll each get three opportunities to try each method for solving the problems. Remember to write your name and method on each problem.

At that point, most of the students go to work, and Ms. Anderson invites the four students who answered the group question incorrectly to join her at the table in the center of the room. At various times of the year, every student in the class has worked with Ms. Anderson at the center table, receiving guided instruction while the rest of the class completed productive group work. When the four students arrive at the table, Ms. Anderson introduces a new problem:

Ms. Anderson: So, let's try to work a really hard one, shall we?

Students: Yeah!

Ms. Anderson: OK. Let's look at this one, number 9. "A glass jar contains six red, five green, eight blue, and three yellow marbles. If a single marble is chosen at random from the jar, what is the probability of choosing a red marble? A green marble?" Wow, that's a lot of information! How might we set this up?

Michael: Well, there are six red ones, so one out of six.

Ms. Anderson: You're partly right. Let's talk about this some more. You are going to choose one marble, so you're right on, there. But how many red marbles are there?

Michael: Six.

Ms. Anderson: So when you pick a marble, you have six chances to get red, right?

Sarah: But you're only getting one, not six. It says right here.

Ms. Anderson: You are so right; you're only choosing one marble. But how many red marbles are there in the jar? That's how you figure probability.

Sarah: Oh, because you could get pick any one of the six of the reds, right?

Ms. Anderson: Excellent, yes. Michael, can you explain that to Ahmed?

Michael: I guess. So, there is this jar with a bunch of marbles. There are six red marbles in there, so when you pick, you have six chances to pick a red one.

Ahmed: Yeah, I get that. The numerator is 6. But I don't know how to get the denominator.

Jessica: For me, that's the easy part. It's the total. The jar has 22 marbles in it. I added up the numbers of red, green, blue, and yellow, and there are 22. What I don't get is why they say "random." If the jar is glass, I can see the marbles and just get a red one.

Ahmed: But maybe it's the kind of glass you can't see through. Then you have to figure it out.

Michael: So 22 is the denominator? Then it's 6/22, right?

Jessica: You forgot to reduce. You can't have a fraction like that.

Sarah: I got 3/11 reduced. How's that?

Ms. Anderson: Did anyone get another number? Let's check. No? So we all got 3/11 for the chance of a red one. How about a green one?

While Ms. Anderson engages these four students in guided instruction, the rest of the class members continue to work in their groups of three. When she finishes with this small-group guided lesson, she joins other small groups at work and checks their understanding. Although she sees that the triad of Jeff, Kara, and Mark was able to solve the problems with numbers and illustrations, all three students seem to struggle with expressing their solution to her in words. Using a similar line of questioning she used with the group at the center table, Ms. Anderson guides Jeff, Kara, and Mark though the learning:

Ms. Anderson: OK, so instead of starting by writing things down, why don't we start by talking about one of the problems? Jeff, do you want to read number 4?

Jeff: OK, it says, "Annie rolls a single six-sided die. What is the probability she will roll an even number?"

Ms. Anderson: Great. Well, I see you already have the answer, and you've illustrated it. Talk about how you solved this problem.

Kara: Well, I started by asking myself how many even numbers a die has, and said three.

Ms. Anderson: Excellent. So how would you write that in words?

Jeff: A die has three even numbers: a two, a four, and a six?

Ms. Anderson: OK, write that down. Mark, what did you do next?

Mark: I knew that there were six sides all together, so that would make it three chances out of six that the girl would roll an even number. And three over six is the same as one-half. So I'd write that down.

Kara: Oh, I've got it. This isn't so hard. We could also say that there is a one out of six chance she will roll a two, plus a one out of six chance that she'll roll a four, plus a one out of six chance she'll roll a six . . . which is three out of six.

Jeff: Which is the same as one-half. OK, I got it. Let's try the next one.

In the process of explaining their thinking out loud, the students were able to build on and clarify each other's thinking. Jeff, Kara, and Mark together knew more than any one of them knew alone. Ms. Anderson did not give these students the answer; she merely created the conditions for collaborative learning and primed the pump. Now, as they complete the task, she sees that they will soon be ready for independent work related to probability.

And that's what this book is about—engaging students in productive group work that allows them practice with content and opportunities to consolidate their understanding as they proceed toward independent learning. Productive group work also provides teachers with opportunities to reteach those students in need of additional instruction without sacrificing the whole class. In other words, productive group work is an important part of the gradual release of responsibility, which facilitates student competence and independence.

1

Defining Productive Group Work

Educators since Socrates have known that knowledge is built and extended through the exchange of ideas and that students should be encouraged to question and push each other's understanding. Today, technological advancements have made it possible even for people separated by continents to learn and work collaboratively. In a dramatic example, physician Jerri Nielsen, while based at Amundsen-Scott South Pole Station, was able to use Web-based technology to confer with doctors in Indiana. Together they diagnosed and planned treatment of Nielsen's breast cancer until she could be airlifted from the station. But whether people collaborate across a tabletop or a digital landscape, the elements of successful productive group work remain the same, as does its ultimate end: *a useful result.* In a school setting, that result is a new understanding or outcome that leads to academic and social growth.

The Basis of Group Work Today

Although group work has been used in teaching for thousands of years, it really wasn't until the 1970s and the work of Lev Vygotsky that groups were widely recognized as key to the learning process. Perhaps the most influential theorist on the role of peer-assisted learning, Vygotsky drew the world's attention to the vital importance of collaboration. He proposed that "every function in the child's cultural development appears twice: first, on the social level, and later, on the individual level; first, between people . . . and then inside the child" (1978, p. 57). In other words, learning is social. What children learn through social interactions with adults and peers forms the basis for more complex thinking and understanding. Over time, these skills, learning, and thinking processes become internalized and can be used independently. In short, by interacting with others, children learn not only what to think but *how* to think.

Vygotsky believed all learning to be the product of sociocultural phenomena, mediated by interactions with others (Berk & Winsler, 1995), or that the learner's view of the world is shaped by social interactions. Without the benefit of an expanded view, a student's learning is limited by the range of his or her experiences. Thus, interactions with peers expand a student's aptitude for seeking new information. With this assertion, collaboration with peers becomes a necessary part of the learning process of a child. Indeed, Vygotsky identified both the teacher and peers as important agents in the process (Crain, 2005). In this light, we must view group work as more than a means of completing a project or task. Productive group work is an essential stepping stone to learning and mastery.

But as we discussed in the Introduction, group work can go wrong and often does. Even if we recognize that group learning is vital for our students, simply placing them in groups and giving them a task does not mean learning or mastery is soon to follow. Conditions must be right. In their seminal work *Learning Together and Alone,* David Johnson and Roger Johnson (1975) identified many of the conditions necessary for successful group work. They defined cooperative learning as an instructional arrangement that allows two to six students the opportunity to work together on a shared task in order to jointly construct their knowledge and understanding of the content. Johnson and Johnson's five principles for making the arrangement successful—*positive interdependence, face-to-face interaction, individual and group accountability, interpersonal and small-group skills,* and *group processing*—have since become well known to multiple generations of teachers.

Still, although most elementary and middle school teachers report featuring cooperative learning in their classrooms, many also confess to struggling with how to support the peer interactions within the groups (Antil, Jenkins, Wayne, &

Vadasy, 1998; Tomlinson, Moon, & Callahan, 1997). In the chapters to come, we will examine each of Johnson and Johnson's principles in detail, offering a rationale for why each principle is important, routines to ensure each principle is incorporated in group work, and classroom examples of how teachers can best support students in groups. To start, we would like to present a brief overview of Johnson and Johnson's five elements and an account of how one teacher uses them in her classroom to make group work productive.

Positive Interdependence

To create positive interdependence within groups, the group task must be designed so that the participation of every member is necessary to its completion, and students must clearly understand their interdependence in accomplishing the task. The task should also capitalize on the variation among group members so that individual strengths can be tapped. Johnson and Johnson (1994) observed that interdependence may be accomplished in the following four ways:

1. *Goals* can be made interdependent by assigning a task that requires each member to contribute for the group to be successful. In other words, they sink or swim together.

2. *Resources* can be distributed to ensure each group member has a unique piece of information essential for completing a task, and no one can complete the task alone or without each member's contribution.

3. *Rewards* are excellent motivators for interdependence when given both for individual contribution to the group task and for the overall group effort and result. Group members then know they have a stake in each other's learning and their own.

4. *Roles* can be assigned to give each group member a distinct way to participate in the group's work. Each member's job should be necessary to completing the task. Some common roles are recorder, materials manager, encourager, and reporter.

In the Classroom. Fourth grade teacher Theresa Czarnopys and her students at East Oakview School in Northview, Michigan, regularly use productive group work to consolidate and extend their understanding of texts. Ms. Czarnopys calls the group activity she designed for this purpose "Cube-It." After students have completed a common reading, they move to their collaborative groups to discuss six questions that encourage them to create meaning from the text. Group members take turns rolling a die to determine the order in which the questions are addressed. Each number on the die corresponds to one of the six questions. If the first student rolls a 3, she is the discussion leader and note taker for that question. For example, after reading a text about the California Gold Rush, the groups met to roll the die to discuss the following questions:

1. *Describe It:* In one year's time, San Francisco grew from a city of 900 people to a whopping 56,000 people! Describe how this growth happened so quickly, giving as many details as possible.

2. *Analyze It:* What were some of the problems that resulted from such a huge growth in the number of people in California during the Gold Rush?

3. *Apply It:* Many people came to California as a way to "get rich quick" but had no intention of mining gold. What were some of the different ways that people made lots of money as a result of the Gold Rush?

4. *Take a Stand:* Do you think it is better to get rich quickly or to stick to a slower but safer method of making money? Why?

5. *Reinvent It:* If you had lived during the Gold Rush period, what ideas might you have had to make money without having to mine the gold?

6. *Choose a Different Perspective:* Do you think you would have tried to convince your parents to move the family to California to search for gold, or would you have argued against it? Why?

Of course, these questions could be answered independently, but Ms. Czarnopys knows that the students can better clarify and expand their understanding of the content by using and building on the ideas of peers. She ensures participation of each group member by using a "down-and-up" discussion routine. ("Down and up" refers to going around the table to give each student a chance to speak.) Each member of the group folds a piece of paper into six sections and takes notes as others speak. The discussion leader creates a bulleted list of notes that captures the key ideas and main points for each question. These notes become a visible record of the group's collective thinking and also provide each member of the group with a record of his or her own thinking and the thinking of other members of the group. The students know that after their group discussion, groups will be asked to participate in a whole-class discussion of the topic, during which any member of a group may be asked to answer any of the six Cube-It questions. Students clearly understand that the goal is for all to participate and be able to discuss the content. Additionally, knowing that their reward, or group grade, will depend on Ms. Czarnopys's observation of their group discussion and on their performance in the whole-class discussion, they are motivated to include all members in their group talks. One of her students commented, "This is the first time everybody listened to my ideas—even Michael!"

Face-to-Face Interaction

To consolidate and build new understanding, groups need to have considerable face-to-face interaction. Importantly, these interactions should be designed to encourage the exchange of ideas and not just to work out the logistics of completing the assignment. While interaction may seem to be a given of group work, we've seen groups avoid this element by merely splitting up work on a task and agreeing to put the individual pieces together as a whole. For example, we've watched groups assigned to create a PowerPoint presentation quickly divide the work and go off to separate computers to create a few slides. They did come back together to assemble the slides, but without discussion of the concepts contained in the presentation. When the time came to present, the students talked about the slides they made. When questioned, none of the students could address any part of the topic except the one he or she had personally worked on.

To be sure, new technologies are pushing the boundaries of face-to-face interaction. Doug, Nancy, and Sandi are all advocates of technology that promotes learning, and we will address the use of social technology tools, such as Twitter, for group work in Chapter 3.

In the Classroom. Two design elements of the Cube-It activity Ms. Czarnopys used to ensure interdependence also promote face-to-face interaction. Because she requires that each student in the group be prepared to answer any of the six questions during the whole-class discussion, group members must interact and share their ideas to make sure everyone is prepared. They cannot simply divide the questions, making individuals responsible for knowing the answer to one or two questions. The down-and-up routine also ensures every student has a chance to contribute. To keep some students from dominating, Ms. Czarnopys says she "limits the time for critical conversations so that students stay on task." In addition, she supports the interaction of students who may have trouble contributing to the discussion about a particular question by giving them comprehension cue cards.

Individual and Group Accountability

As teachers, our concern is that each student learn, and for this we need to create an accountability system that provides feedback to the individual learner as well as to the group. Teachers often assign both an individual and a group grade for a group task. The key to this accountability system is that the members of the group are aware that each individual will receive a grade and that each is a participant in the evaluation process. Each group member may provide feedback on his or her own performance and the work of others. Johnson and Johnson (1994) also suggest that a group "checker" be identified to ask each member to explain the group's work or responses.

In the Classroom. Ms. Czarnopys holds students accountable for both their group interactions and their individual learning. Students receive a group grade based on their group's performance in the whole-class discussion. Ms. Czarnopys also visits each group as they work on the Cube-It activity and evaluates individual work. She makes notes about participation and engagement, and she listens for evidence of contributions from each member. It's not uncommon to hear her say to a student discussion leader, "I really liked the point so-and-so just made. Could you put her initials next to that comment on your bulleted list?"

She also considers the content of their dialogue as she listens for misconceptions or inaccurate assumptions. This monitoring allows her to scaffold for meaning when a group is stuck on a discussion question.

Additionally, Ms. Czarnopys gives students an individual writing assignment that she uses as part of her assessment system. The thematic focus of the unit, which included the Gold Rush, was on the difference between wishes and dreams, and another text students read and discussed was Alma Flor Ada's 1994 narrative *The Gold Coin.* Using what they had learned about wishes and dreams from the California Gold Rush text and the narrative piece, she asked them to write individually about the positive and negative aspects of a dream that comes true.

Interpersonal and Small-Group Skills

Group work should promote frequent use of interpersonal and small-group skills. These are some of the applied skills held in such high regard by employers, and they include the ability to resolve conflicts in a constructive manner, to communicate effectively, and to ably draw upon the strengths of others to solve problems. Although they are young, students in classrooms that feature productive group work are learning each day how to organize and coordinate efforts and are acquiring a results-oriented outlook that will serve them well through years to come.

These valuable skills can be taught and practiced using a *helping curriculum* (Sapon-Shevin, 1998). Students in classrooms that emphasize this approach learn how to offer help to others ("Can I help you find the right chapter?") as well as how to accept such offers ("Yes, can you give me a hand?"). Learners also need to know when and how to request assistance from others ("I don't understand this. Could you explain it to me?"). Often overlooked, but certainly critical, is the skill of declining assistance with grace ("I'd like to try it again first, but I appreciate the offer"). At the heart of practicing interpersonal skills is the reality that all of us are, at different times, givers *and* receivers of help. Reciprocity in supporting one another is essential if students are to reach productive results.

In the Classroom. Because her students use the Cube-It activity routinely, throughout the year Ms. Czarnopys witnesses growth in the interpersonal skills of each of her students. She has been especially pleased with the effect the many opportunities to practice these skills has had on quieter students. She often sees that while these students may be reluctant at the beginning of the year to offer help, by the end of the year, they are doing so more freely. In some cases, encouraging these students to engage is a matter of fostering self-confidence, while in other cases it may require that students be more cognizant of their need for assistance from others. Ms. Czarnopys notes that "in small groups, quieter students are more willing to share, particularly once a conversation has started and ideas begin to flow."

Group Processing

Although it's the most easily overlooked of all the elements of cooperative learning, frequent and regular group processing is the key to a group's future effectiveness. Teachers often forget to include this step in their group work design. And even when it is incorporated, in the rush to finish the project, turn in the assignment, and hurry off to the next class, students can easily shortchange assessing their work as a group. However, the opportunity for groups to talk to one another about what worked and what didn't is crucial to future success. It's not a matter of blaming individuals but, rather, of figuring out what should change and what should be retained. Educators know that the complex task of school improvement requires the analysis of successes and areas that need improvement. In the same way, learners need an opportunity to notice what they did well and what got in the way.

In the Classroom. Ms. Czarnopys routinely collects feedback from students about their roles in Cube-It groups. She asks them to discuss what was easy and what was hard about the task and to think about the ways they contributed to the process. In addition, she leads classroom discussions to gather evidence of positive contributions. Students may offer examples of a group member who made an important realization that got the group "unstuck" or of a time when a classmate offered assistance to the group by taking the lead on an aspect of the task. Ms. Czarnopys commented that "collaborative work allows for clarifying thinking at all levels of comprehension." Reflecting on Cube-It, one of her students summed up the benefits of productive group work this way: "I like to work in groups—it makes me feel smarter!"

Providing a Meaningful Task

To Johnson and Johnson's five principles of cooperative learning, we would like to add a sixth: *a meaningful task.* A task for productive group work must offer a challenge or a problem to solve to make all of those principles of cooperative learning come into play. Why does a looming problem make for better group work? Because it's the wrestling with a task that causes students to rely on one another. A spirit of cooperation can bloom when a group is collectively faced with a difficult job to do.

Let's take an everyday example: merging into traffic. You are in your car in heavy traffic on the highway and a lane is ending. Cars are jockeying for position as they squeeze over. Chances are you are either what writer Cynthia Gorney (2008) calls a "lineupper" or a "sidezoomer." The lineuppers, who are patiently waiting their turn, typically don't want to let those rude sidezoomers into the lane. The sidezoomers, on the other hand, are using the available space to get ahead, never mind the line. So how does the problem resolve?

Because we all understand or have experienced the consequences of failing to cooperatively queue—accidents, horns honking, or road rage—we are motivated to work together to avoid these outcomes. When the traffic's moving along smoothly, we really don't notice our fellow drivers. But when merging lanes loom ahead, we start to pay attention to them and to work together, cooperatively queuing with a minimum of braking and speeding up, to ensure everyone gets in the lane and all can move ahead. Students, too, need to have the potential of failure to make them pay attention to each other and what they are doing and to figure out how they might work together toward success. If success is guaranteed, the task is not likely to result in learning.

You will recall from the Introduction that collaborative learning should occur when students are ready to tackle a challenge: after a purpose has been established, modeling has been provided, and they have had sufficient guided practice. If it's too early in the instructional cycle, students are going to give up. But if the timing is right, students will engage. The teacher is there at the elbow of learners to scaffold, but it's acceptable to delay the question, cue, or prompt for just a bit to let them try to sort it out. In fact, there is an entire research base on the importance of "productive failure" as an essential element of productive group learning (e.g., Kapur, 2008). It seems that when the task is structured so that it is difficult, but not impossible, learners actually outperform those who were in groups that had tasks that ensured success. Groups truly need a problem that might result in an incorrect answer, a failed experiment, or inaccurate conclusion.

In the Classroom. Consider how Theresa Czarnopys structures productive group work with the fearless confidence of an educator who knows that her students need time to wrestle with difficulty and risk possible failure. She deliberately constructed a challenging task. Her Cube-It questions ("Do you think it is better to get rich quickly or to stick to a slower but safer method of making money? Why?") cannot be answered with a pat reply. These kinds of questions also make it unlikely that group members will reach the same conclusions, and so they generate comparison and debate—discussion! And, although she monitors the groups' progress, she strategically delays using cues, questions, and prompts to let the students figure out what they think. She explains that she has to remember to "allow students the opportunity to create meaning from the questions and not to be too quick to tell them what the question is asking." In other words, she recognizes the productivity of possible failure because she trusts the process of collaborative learning and knows that the gradual release of responsibility will result in increased student learning. "For me," she says, "there is no better learning for students than that which they take on themselves and from each other."

A Few Thoughts on Differentiation and Productive Group Work

The issue of task difficulty during productive group work can tempt teachers into reverting to ability grouping. Resist the urge. As we noted in the Introduction, the group tends to be wiser than the individual. The differentiation that occurs in this phase of instruction is accompanied by the scaffolding that peers are able to provide for one another; these are not individual tasks. Consider, then, that productive group work is a critical phase that occurs within a larger differentiated classroom experience.

Meet the Teachers

Throughout the book, we will peek inside different classrooms to see how teachers are incorporating the elements of cooperative learning to make their groups productive. However, there are three educators we will visit regularly at the end of each chapter. Let's introduce them now: Aida Allen, Kathy Vogel, and Brian Gibbs.

Aida Allen is an elementary teacher in San Diego, California, who has had the rare opportunity to do what educators in previous centuries took for granted—teach the same group of students from kindergarten through 5th grade. All of her students speak Spanish as their first language and are enrolled in a bilingual program designed to build literacy skills in both Spanish and English. In the following chapters, you will see how Ms. Allen uses collaborative learning to build the social and academic language skills of her students.

Kathy Vogel is a 7th grade English and social studies teacher in Northview, Michigan. Although the students in this suburban community are native English speakers, they also need the oral and written experiences that come with productive group work. Across the next five chapters, you will read about an innovative research project Ms. Vogel's students complete together to deepen their understanding of world events.

Brian Gibbs teaches high school social studies in Los Angeles, California, at one of the largest high schools in the country. Although his classes frequently exceed 40 students per class, Mr. Gibbs uses group work to create a classroom where students' understanding of history is regularly on display as student groups reenact historical events, characters, and culture.

We hope the glimpses inside these teachers' classrooms will illuminate the process of collaborative learning and demonstrate the potential of productive group work: what your students may achieve socially and academically, and how you can support them in that learning.

2

Using Positive Interdependence

Many hands make light work. English poet John Heywood was probably not think-ing about productive group work when he wrote these words in 1546, but he undoubtedly had some end result in mind. A key feature of productive group work is what Johnson and Johnson (1975) call *positive interdependence*. In fact, positive interdependence is considered by many to be the defining quality and most impor-tant component of cooperative group work.

When established successfully, positive interdependence results in students' rec-ognizing that their individual success is inextricably linked to the success of every other member of the group. This realization only occurs when the accomplishment of a group task requires more than just segmenting the work into smaller pieces for members to do alone. The structure of the task must demand that each member of the group offer a unique contribution to the joint effort. When students perceive that every member is indispensable to achieving their mutual goals and that they are both dependent on and obligated to their peers, conditions are ripe for collab-orative learning.

What Students Are Learning About Themselves

We all want to contribute something unique, to have an important role, to be valued by others, and students are no exception. If group work is designed to be interdependent, these needs are met, and the resulting positive atmosphere allows learning to take place. As we have noted, productive group work is ultimately about results. It is important to remember, however, that outcomes are not just about task completion. Students who mistakenly think that the only thing the teacher cares about is whether the job is done are missing out on the learning that occurs in the process. Teachers who foster a false dichotomy of complete versus incomplete tasks are overlooking the nuances of what happens inside the mind of learners as they work in tandem with others.

In collaborative work, there is always a tension between two types of learning. Hulse-Killacky, Killacky, and Donigian (2001) describe these as *process learning* and *content learning*. The process questions students are posing to themselves include

- Who am I?

- Who am I with you?

- Who are we together?

And the content questions they are asking include

- What do we have to do?

- What do we need to do to accomplish our goals? (p. 9)

In seeking out the answers to content questions, students have an opportunity to consolidate academic knowledge, but in working out process questions, they gain an understanding of themselves as learners and members of a team. Indeed, an important outcome of productive group work is that learners gain greater metacognitive awareness—that is, self-knowledge of how and when they learn something new.

The key is for students' understanding about themselves to be affirming. They are not going to have a positive picture of themselves as learners if they are not contributors to achieving the group goal. If students realize that they are not full participants, their self-talk is likely to turn negative: *I can't do this because I'm too stupid.* Fear of failure and embarrassment then creeps into the learning process and can form an invisible barrier. We teachers can't see this roadblock, and our students often cannot or will not articulate what has gotten in their way.

The Neural Basis of Positive Interdependence

Many teachers know of the affective filter hypothesis, which proposes that certain emotions can act as filters in the flow of academic learning. Negative feelings, such as fear and embarrassment, can interfere with a learner's ability to process information. In a psychological equivalent to the physiological fight-or-flight response to a threat, a student who experiences negative emotions during learning will either seek escape or freeze up. Learning still takes place, but it is all directed at the threat itself. On the other hand, students experiencing positive emotions have an improved flow of academic information and a heightened state of learning.

Ongoing neuroscience research also supports the idea that emotions affect learning. Current study of the amygdalae, a pair of almond-shaped neuronal clusters located deep in the temporal lobes of the human brain, suggests that its chief functions are to process learning formed through emotional events (especially fear and reward) and to further consolidate these memories as they move from working memory (short in duration) to long-term (more permanent) memory (Howard, 2006). It is this pathway function of the amygdalae that is important in learning. While the thalamus serves as the sensory pathway to various parts of the brain, the amygdalae similarly process emotionally charged events.

Think of the amygdalae as the revolving door of a busy office building (the brain). People flow in and out of the building all day long and travel to various floors depending on the nature of their business. However, this revolving door is a special one, equipped with a security system that vigilantly watches for any sign of threat. When a danger is perceived, the revolving door locks shut, temporarily stopping the flow of traffic. The revolving door's security system collects data so that it can recognize similar threats in the future, creating a "wanted poster" to remind itself not to be fooled again. Similarly, the revolving door's security system also prioritizes the big shots who might be approaching the entry. Let's say the building owner's name is Mr. Reward. Whenever Mr. Reward is spotted walking up the sidewalk, the revolving door makes sure that he is able to enter the building quickly and is whisked up the elevator to his destination. Mr. Reward's pathway is cleared so that nothing will delay his travel to any place in the building.

Perceived threat interferes with academic learning because attention and memory shift to the negative stimuli. Group work that is structured to create positive interdependence reduces threats and increases a sense of reward. When students engaged in group work answer the process learning questions "Who am I?" and

"Who am I with you?" with the answer, "I am a contributor, and we are a team," their level of fear lowers. And when a student anticipates success by answering the content question "What do we have to do?" with "We are figuring out what to do. We are making progress," the pathways open for academic learning. Notice that the reward doesn't have to be external (e.g., grades or praise); learners can intrinsically reward themselves when they experience progress toward an identified goal.

Productive group work can open the doors to learning once students realize that they can rely upon one another to learn complex material. Teachers can foster a sense of positive interdependence by creating tasks that require shared goals, outcomes, and rewards. The esprit de corps that emerges when a group of learners sets goals and collectively experiences success results in gains in their social, emotional, and academic growth.

Instructional Routines That Foster Positive Interdependence

One of the most beneficial aspects of productive group work is that it allows students and teachers to capitalize on the unique skills and capabilities they possess. The naturally occurring variance among learners is often what leads team members to rely upon one another. Heterogeneous grouping may seem to make creating interdependence especially challenging: Each student is more skilled in some ways, less skilled in others. However, these differences do not have to be an impediment; they can become a genuine aid to learning.

Of course, students need help discovering each other's value. Positive interdependence doesn't just happen. Teachers must model and implement routines to promote relationships that encourage rather than inhibit learning. We have found that three instructional routines in particular are useful for fostering interdependence in group work: creating different experiences, using a jigsaw approach, and student-led reciprocal teaching.

Different Experiences

One way to ensure that each group member has something unique and valuable to contribute is to give each a different task. Karen Auppelee, who teaches a blended 1st and 2nd grade class at East Oakview Elementary in Northview, Michigan, often sets up different experiences within her lessons to make the most of productive group work and to manage the different readiness levels typical in a multi-age learning scenario. For example, her 1st grade students spent a day with another classroom, while her 2nd grade students went on a field trip to a sculpture garden in a nearby town. The following day, the whole class worked in mixed-age pairs (one 1st grader and one 2nd grader) to compare their experiences through discussion, drawing, and writing. Because each partner possessed information the other did not, they had to engage in real dialogue about the events to complete the tasks. As the discussions progressed, each pair created Venn diagrams of the similarities and differences between their experiences. For example, Natalie and Karen agreed that they "both had yummy lunches" and "hope they can do it again!" Ashley and Zoe noted, "Both of us went outside." Then the groups used the jointly constructed graphic organizer as a basis for their writing assignment. Each set of students collaboratively wrote two or three paragraphs on how they spent their day.

During the partner group work, Ms. Auppelee provided guided instruction and collected assessment information. "I was able to assess their understanding by listening to their discussions and observing how they worked together," she later remarked. "It was evident that learning took place because they were identifying other compare and contrast writings and suggesting other activities that we could do for [this kind] of writing!"

The Jigsaw Approach

Jigsaw is a commonly used method of promoting interdependence (Aronson, Blaney, Sikes, Stephan, & Snapp, 1978). In this approach, a complex learning task is split among group members. Each student is simultaneously a member of two groups: a *home group,* whose chief goal is to learn the content and complete tasks, and an *expert group,* which consists of one representative member from each home group. Students meet in their home group to discuss overall goals. Then they meet in their expert group to focus on one specific aspect of the content. After mastering the expert content, each member returns to his or her home group to teach that element to the rest of the group (see Figure 2.1).

Because the home group's success depends on each member's expertise, it is important to make sure that all students are adequately learning the material so they can share information accurately. Teacher monitoring of the expert groups is critical, especially when the process is new to the class. And ensuring mastery may present a challenge because students are at different readiness levels. On the one hand, a student working below grade level may take a bit longer to learn the content.

Figure 2.1	A Jigsaw Arrangement: Home and Expert Groups

Phase 1: Students meet in home groups.

1	2
3	4

1	2
3	4

1	2
3	4

1	2
3	4

Phase 2: Students meet in expert groups.

1	1
1	1

2	2
2	2

3	3
3	3

4	4
4	4

Phase 3: Students return to home groups to teach one another.

1	2
3	4

1	2
3	4

1	2
3	4

1	2
3	4

On the other hand, a student who is already an expert on a topic may become impatient with other members of her group. It may be helpful to assign these more knowledgeable students as group leaders so that they can facilitate the process. Let them know that practicing is an essential part of learning and that it can and should occur. The teacher should also check the accuracy and completeness of each student's learning in the expert group before they return to their home groups. When students of differing abilities feel well supported in a jigsaw arrangement, there is a positive effect on motivation (Shaaban, 2006).

The originator of jigsaw grouping, psychologist Eliot Aronson, had another goal in mind when he came up with the jigsaw method. In his book *Nobody Left to Hate,* Aronson (2000) describes how in 1971 he and his graduate students devised the jigsaw classroom as a way to defuse the racial tensions present at a school in Austin, Texas, that was the first in the district to desegregate. Learners were given complex tasks that required them to lean on each other in order to be successful. He described one group's realization regarding their treatment of a boy named Carlos, an English learner in their home group, who had just learned about Eleanor Roosevelt in his expert group:

> One of my research assistants was observing that group and heard some members of Carlos's group make remarks such as, "Aw, you don't know it, you're dumb, you're stupid." . . . Instead of admonishing them to "be nice" or "try to cooperate," she made one simple but powerful statement. "Talking like that to Carlos might be fun for you to do, but it's not going to help you learn anything about Eleanor Roosevelt . . . and the exam will be in about fifteen minutes." (p. 142)

Aronson goes on to explain that "Carlos's groupmates gradually realized that they needed to change their tactics. It was no longer in their best interest to rattle Carlos; he wasn't the enemy—he was on their team" (p. 143).

Although most of our classrooms today do not harbor the same dramatic tensions present in 1971, the marginalization of classmates is still a routine occurrence, as is its consequent negative effect on academic learning. The point isn't that everyone should somehow become friends, but that when students learn that they need one another, they begin to appreciate the strengths others possess.

Interdependence also has valuable long-term social benefits. The ability for people to work productively with others is an adult outcome that predicts whether a person will remain employed. A longitudinal study of over 10,000 high school students 10 years after graduation found that those who had been rated higher by their teachers on the ability to relate to others had achieved a higher level of post-secondary education and higher annual income than those rated lower on social skills, even when controlled for cognitive skills (Lieras, 2008).

It's worth noting that jigsaw's home group work mirrors the multidisciplinary work that is the hallmark of many professional fields, including medicine, law, education, and business. At one time or another, all of us have been members of a work group assembled to achieve a complex goal, with members selected because each possesses specialized knowledge about a particular aspect of the problem. In these situations, no one member is expected to come up with the solution; it's assumed the solution will arise from the interaction of the whole group. In the classroom, as in the adult work world, jigsawing can foster both individual expertise and interdependence, as members come together to create a new solution.

Student-Led Reciprocal Teaching

Another way teachers can encourage positive interdependence is through *reciprocal teaching,* or asking group members to assume specific roles when considering a problem. As working adults, we participate in reciprocal teaching each time we gather to plan how to complete a project. After analyzing the task, we discuss what must be done and figure out who will do what. Similarly, reciprocal teaching requires students to work together to achieve a task-related goal. Together, they learn that "sometimes there are several different ways of saying the same thing and that there are many right answers to the same question" (Palincsar, Ransom, & Derber, 1988/1989, p. 38).

The interactive instructional process known as reciprocal teaching is often used in group work focusing on reading comprehension. The group task is to reach an understanding of a text, and each of the four group members is assigned a role that matches a comprehension strategy: generating questions, summarizing content, clarifying key points, and making predictions about what the author will discuss next. The group discusses the text with each student contributing based on his or her role. Every member of the group is expected to participate and, in fact, needs to participate in order for the group to construct meaning. Students may find task cards helpful as reminders of how to fulfill their role in discussion. Here are some examples of role prompts:

Questioner

1. Ask a question that can be answered in the text (a Right There or Think and Search question).
2. Ask an opinion question (Do you agree? What do you think?).
3. Show your teammates where you find answers.

Clarifier

1. Ask if anyone got stuck on a word or an idea.
2. Help your teammates by using resources. Try rereading first.
3. If the person is stuck on a word, try the glossary or dictionary.
4. If these don't work, ask for help from the teacher.

Predictor

1. Tell your teammates what you think the author will tell you about in the next section.
2. Show your teammates the clues you noticed in the passage.

Summarizer

1. Tell your teammates the main idea of the passage and the important supporting details.
2. Make sure your summary isn't longer than the reading!

Reciprocity of teaching and learning is vital to this instructional routine and is an important aspect for the teacher to model. Initially, teachers demonstrate each comprehension strategy. Using a think-aloud technique (Davey, 1983) that allows teachers to make their thinking explicit as they make sense of a passage is effective. For example, teachers read a paragraph aloud and then talk about the questions that occur to them as they read. This technique shows that all readers ask questions of themselves during the reading process. Students then take turns assuming the role of the teacher as they lead their small group in conversation about the text. Over time—Palincsar, Ransom, and Derber (1988/1989) recommend about 20 lessons—students are equipped to engage in reciprocal teaching within productive work groups. Teachers may assign roles, or the groups may do so themselves. In our experience, as groups become more comfortable with the discussion process, they become increasingly comfortable assuming different roles, resulting in further consolidation of sound reading comprehension and monitoring strategies.

Inside Three Classrooms

As we mentioned in Chapter 1, four types of interdependence can be built into group work: goal, resource, reward, and role. The following classroom examples show how some of the routines discussed can link students in learning and what kinds of positive interdependence these routines create.

Ms. Allen, Elementary School Science

You may recall that Ms. Aida Allen taught the same students from kindergarten through the 5th grade. When her students were in 4th grade, she introduced them to reciprocal teaching. For several weeks, her students worked on learning the different strategy roles used in reading comprehension group work. For instance, Ms. Allen would model a role, such as clarifying, during whole-class focus lessons and then follow up with guided reading instruction to further refine students' skills. As students became more skilled with each role, she began to combine different roles to build their capacity for sustaining the discussion. After students had mastered generating questions and summarizing, Ms. Allen had them use both to read a short piece of text. "It's about building stamina," she remarked. "I want them to get comfortable with doing more on their own."

After the several weeks of practice, Ms. Allen felt that her students were ready to tackle reciprocal teaching in small groups. One day, in science, she assigned them to groups of four, with a member responsible for each role: questioning, clarifying, summarizing, and predicting. Groups were given a passage on decomposers that complemented information found in their science textbook. Ms. Allen segmented the reading into shorter passages, and the students knew they were to have a discussion at the end of each segment. In case they got stuck, she put task tent cards that listed prompting questions for each role on each group's table.

Here's what happened in one group:

> *Tino:* OK, I'll go first. I'm the summarizer, so I'm supposed to say the main idea. So here goes. The main idea is that when plants and animals die, they get decomposed. That means they get eaten by stuff, and they turn into soil. And the stuff is bacteria, or fungi, or earthworms.
>
> *Miriam:* I'm supposed to ask a question. Do earthworms decompose plants or animals?
>
> *Tino:* They eat plants and animals.
>
> *Miriam:* Right! It says right here [points to text]: "Earthworms decompose dead plants and animals."
>
> *Adriana:* Ask a harder question, Miriam.
>
> *Miriam:* OK. What do you think would happen if there weren't any decomposers?

This question sparked a lively conversation that went on for several minutes as the group debated what the Earth might be like if everything that ever died was still in its original form. This notion had not occurred to them before, and they were quite delighted to speculate about general living conditions and the difficulty of getting around all the dead stuff. This speculation prompted Romel, the clarifier, to ask a question of his own:

> *Romel:* That's something I don't understand. How could everything that ever died be turned just into dirt? Wouldn't we be under piles and piles of dirt?

> *Tino:* You're the clarifier. How can we find the answer?

> Tino rechecked his role card and decided that they needed to ask the teacher. They called Ms. Allen over and presented Romel's question to her. She asked the group if it was possible that they might find the answer to their question in subsequent passages.

> *Adriana:* Oh yeah, that's my job. I forgot about it! Maybe we thought of that question like the author did. At the end of the third paragraph, it says, "Decomposers are an important part of the web of life because without them there would be no plant life. Without plant life, other organisms would no longer exist."

As the group continued to read and discuss the assigned passage, they discovered that decomposers play an important role in passing on energy.

This productive group work demonstrated both *role interdependence* and *goal interdependence*. Each student understood and carried out a unique role in completing the task, and each student had to contribute to achieve the group goal of understanding the text. The group also learned about each other's thinking as they analyzed the text and monitored their understanding. This was an early attempt at reciprocal teaching for Ms. Allen's students; the routine became a regularly featured one in her classroom as they tackled informational reading.

Ms. Vogel, Middle School Humanities

The students in Kathy Vogel's 7th grade humanities class were studying the countries of the eastern hemisphere as part of their yearlong study of world cultures. Ms. Vogel knew that a requirement of her state's standards was for students to plan and deliver focused and coherent informational presentations. To combine their research with this standard, she assigned a project in which partners had to collaborate to write and deliver an interview modeled on the television show *Larry King Live.*

First, the class watched and analyzed portions of several broadcasts to determine the elements of a strong interview; they then composed a rubric to be used with their own projects. Ms. Vogel then modeled with a student an interview she had written. Working from a script, she interviewed a representative from the Tengiz Oil and Gas Refinery in Kazakhstan to highlight information about the physical and economic features of the country. "I realize the importance of modeling meaningful interview questions," Ms. Vogel commented. "Particularly the importance of showing students how to make decisions about what to ask."

The modeling that accompanied this interview project was designed to show students how she utilized her background knowledge and understanding of the task to share her ideas with a partner. The project lent itself to overall positive interdependence (the development and performance of an interview), but Ms. Vogel also made sure that students were individually accountable for the script they developed. She visited each team throughout the script research and writing phase of the project, discussing the viewpoints each partner would be representing during the interview. In addition, she gave students individual grades based on the quality of information furnished by the character each portrayed in the presentation. Ms. Vogel's continued presence throughout the development of the project ensured that each team member was contributing to the overall process.

Student partners brainstormed a list of people, issues, and events related to their assigned regions. Eric and Dave were assigned Israel, and they chose to interview a representative of the Israeli government about the ongoing conflict in the region. Their scripted interview began with a discussion of the formation of Israel after World War II and established the basis for the modern conflict. At one point in their interview, this exchange took place:

> *Eric* (as Larry King): This conflict has been going on for a long time, so when do you think this conflict will end?
>
> *Dave* (as an Israeli government official): Well, being a religious man, I believe this conflict will end once both sides suffer even greater losses and realize they can no longer pay the price for their hatred. This will probably require forces and events that are beyond anything one man can accomplish.

Eric: What will this conflict's lasting significance be?

Dave: Thousands of bright and intelligent people who could have added help to the world have been killed because of this.

The collaborative work between partners to research, compose, rehearse, and perform their interviews fostered a strong level of positive interdependence. Because they had a vested interest in a successful performance, partners helped each other to master the material and concepts.

Mr. Gibbs, High School Social Studies

During each unit of study in Brian Gibbs's American history class, student groups regularly examine historical figures by creating a character analysis for each and participating in a character seminar. For example, at the beginning of their unit on the 10 Cold War presidents, each group was assigned a president and challenged to become an expert on that president's life and administration. Over the next few weeks, the groups learned about their president, such as how he made America safe, his character and leadership style, important choices and decisions he made, and the historical context in which he served. Each member of a group received a prepared packet of different research material, including copies of primary source documents, book excerpts, and articles about the assigned president. This created *resource interdependence,* as students had to study their individual packets and then present what they gleaned to the other members of their group. Each member's input was necessary for the group to develop a complete picture of the president.

In addition to doing an in-depth analysis of their assigned president, each group was required to do a more abbreviated character analysis of the other nine Cold War presidents, based on information gathered from a variety of resources and activities. The "Walk and Talk" activity was a particularly good example of positive interdependence. Students created a graphic organizer and then filled it with information about each president, such as important events in the president's life, key contributions he made in a specific area (e.g., civil rights), and major problems or criticisms he faced during his term in office. Their sources for this information were peers outside their own expert groups. Essentially, the activity consisted of students going up to one another and engaging in a process of "you tell me about your president and I'll tell you about mine." Mr. Gibbs, listening to these conversations, was able to get a good idea of what students knew and what they didn't know yet. Students' completed graphic organizers provided a starting point for further focused reading to support a one-page character analysis of each president.

And at the end of the unit, each group demonstrated their learning by presenting their president in a character seminar and answering questions about their president posed by the rest of the students in the class. This seminar, like all Mr. Gibbs's character seminars, was predominantly student directed, with him stepping in to facilitate only when needed.

Groups prepared for the seminar by reviewing materials together, quizzing each other, and rehearsing responses to likely questions. Every team member had to master the content and be prepared to answer questions. Group members were also responsible for developing high-quality, relevant questions about the other nine presidents, with each group member required to contribute at least two questions for each president. This seminar format created *goal interdependence,* as group members and whole groups pushed one another to analyze, evaluate, and defend their assigned president. How well the team performed depended on every member's knowledge and understanding of their president as well as the quality of the questions they posed to classmates on the other teams.

Because individual as well as group performance was assessed, students experienced *reward interdependence.* Teams were evaluated using a rubric that included criteria about the thoroughness of their character analyses, the accuracy of their responses during the seminar, the quality of the questions they posed, and the balance of contributions from individual group members. Because Mr. Gibbs's students went on to participate in a number of character seminars throughout the year, the rubric also enabled them to measure their growth and progress on the various criteria over time.

3

Promoting Face-to-Face Interaction

In Bernt Capra's 1990 film *Mindwalk,* a politician, a poet, and a brilliant physicist meet by chance in Mont Saint-Michel, France, and engage in a conversation that transforms their thinking about time, philosophy, and the meaning of life. Based on the book *The Turning Point* by Fritjof Capra, the movie follows these highly educated and well-read characters as they search for something they cannot find in books or alone. Only by challenging and building on one another's knowledge are they able to discover new territories for thought. Although as educators we would never advocate for the wholesale abandonment of books, we agree that conversations can yield new insights into our understanding of the world. The purpose of communication, after all, is to convey and obtain meaning.

Teachers know and appreciate the importance and value of students sitting across from one another exchanging ideas. In fact, for many of us, watching students wrestle with ideas, challenge each other, and come to common understandings (or agree to disagree) can be the high point of our day, week, or month. Witnessing these "learning transactions" is a privilege to which few other professionals are privy, and we have a responsibility to provide our students opportunities to engage in them. In a world that offers students an increasing array of technologies that isolate, there is also a growing demand for employees who work well in groups. The best opportunity students have for learning to learn and solve problems with others is in the classroom.

Students' face-to-face interactions give them the chance to support each other academically and personally (Johnson, Johnson, & Holubec, 2008). When students actively invest in and support their groupmates' learning, they are practicing the skills required to be part of an effective learning team. The combination of personal and academic supports that emerge is termed "promotive interactions" (p. 14).

Although teachers also support students' learning, the interaction among groups of students can deepen those students' understanding of themselves. A study of the differences between teacher-led and peer-led discussion groups in 8th grade science found that while students arrived at conceptual understanding more quickly when the teacher was facilitating, the peer-led discussions resulted in more metacognitive statements and queries (Hogan, Nastasi, & Pressley, 1999). Importantly, the peer-led groups did arrive at the same levels of conceptual understanding. However, the process of talking to one another face to face resulted in additional insights into how they learned.

You may be asking why the face-to-face part of student interactions is so important. Can't students write or e-mail or post comments online to stretch and support each other's learning? And we answer, yes, some new technologies can encourage interaction, and we have adopted them in our teaching and group work. For example, Doug and Nancy use an e-platform program extensively in our high school and college teaching to encourage online communication among our students. These discussion boards are asynchronous, meaning users can respond to each other's ideas and questions at any time of the day or night. We use a rubric (see Figure 3.1) to establish our expectations for participating on the discussion board and guide formative assessment. The quality standards provided in this rubric correspond to what makes for productive face-to-face interaction. We also use Twitter to send reminders and updates to our students, and they regularly tweet one another.

However, consider what is missing from interacting via written media—all the information we take in from others that is nonverbal. In a face-to-face conversation, we construct meaning not just from the content of words but also from the gestures, movement, and expressions that our partners or groupmates use. Think about your own behavior when you are talking on the telephone with someone. You may gesticulate and change your facial expressions as you speak and listen, even though the person on the other end of the line can't see you. Even our e-mail habits reflect our

Figure 3.1 Rubric for the Formative Evaluation of Discussion Board Posts

Factor	Exemplary	Proficient	Progressing	Below Standards
Individual's role in the learning community	• Student frequently prompts further discussion of a topic. • Student takes a leadership role in discussions. • Student actively engages in and contributes to collaborative learning. • Student demonstrates awareness of the community's needs.	• Student meets the assigned criteria for contributions to the discussions. • Student interacts freely with and encourages other posters.	• Student responds perfunctorily to the posting and response deadlines. • Student occasionally makes an additional comment. • Student makes a marginal effort to become involved in the community.	• Student does not respond to posts until after the posting deadline. • Student does not make an effort to participate in the learning community as it develops.
Quality and content of initial posts	• Posts demonstrate critical thinking to analyze and relate key points. • Posts use creditable sources in addition to course videos or required readings to make major points.	• Posts relate to the assigned discussion topic and show evidence of critical thinking. • Posts use information from course videos or required readings to support points.	• Posts generally summarize or restate discussion topic components and do not show evidence of higher-order thinking skills. • Posts are off-topic and have little connection to course materials.	• Posts do not relate to the assigned discussion topic. • Posts include irrelevant remarks made with no connection to course videos or required readings.
Quality and content of response posts	• Posts provide specific, constructive, and supportive feedback to extend the thinking of colleagues. • Posts encourage continued and deeper discussion. • Posts offer additional resources or experiences.	• Posts provide specific, constructive, and supportive feedback to colleagues. • Posts cite sources from course videos or required readings. • Posts show evidence of personal learning as a result of the student's interaction with colleagues.	• Posts provide general feedback with little or no connection to course videos or required readings. • Posts show little evidence of personal learning as a result of the student's interaction with colleagues.	• Posts provide agreement without substance or connection to course videos or required reading. • Posts show no evidence of personal learning as a result of the student's interaction with colleagues.
Quality of overall written expression	• Opinions and ideas are clearly, concisely, and effectively written in edited standard English. • APA format is used for citations and the accompanying reference list.	• Opinions and ideas are stated clearly in edited standard English. • APA format is used for citations and accompanying reference list of course-related videos and required reading sources.	• Expression is unclear or interrupted by errors. • APA formatting is not used correctly or consistently.	• Expression is unacceptable. • APA format is not used.

Source: Adapted from rubrics created and used by the Master's in Education faculty in the Richard W. Riley College of Education and Leadership, Walden University. Used with permission.

need to assign meaning to our words. The use of emoticons (those little smiley faces used within e-mail messages) is widespread. Short message service (SMS) programs used for text messaging and instant messaging routinely include graphical images to represent a range of facial expressions. Receiving these nonverbal signals is important to our understanding each other and may be an important step in learning.

The Neural Basis of Face-to-Face Interactions

Have you ever found yourself caught up in the contagion of a yawn? Perhaps you were sitting in a faculty meeting when a colleague began to yawn. Before you knew it, you were yawning too. You might have noticed or recall from your undergraduate communications course that people who are talking to each other often unconsciously adopt the gestures and body language of each other to synchronize their conversation. You can see this phenomenon at any local gathering place where people are striking up conversations.

This mirroring behavior has roots in the workings of the brain and may be key to how we learn. In the 1980s, neuroscientist Giacomo Rizzolatti and his colleagues at the University of Parma made a chance discovery. While recording brain activity in macaque monkeys, they noted that specific neurons would fire when the monkey picked up a peanut. What surprised the team was the discovery that the exact same neurons fired when the monkey watched a researcher pick up a peanut. It didn't stop there. The neurons that fired when the monkey watched the researcher eat the peanut were the same as when the monkey himself ate a peanut. Researchers named the neurons that are activated through direct experience *or* by watching someone else have that experience "mirror neurons" (Rizzolatti & Craighero, 2004).

What does this have to do with productive group work? There is emerging evidence that mirror neuron systems might account for humans' ability to read the facial signals or body language of others and to feel empathy. For example, a recent study showed that the same olfactory portion of the brain became activated when human subjects personally smelled a disgusting odor as when they observed an actor making a disgusted face. When looking at and imitating different facial expressions, magnetic resonance imaging (MRI) of the brain activity of children with and without autism (a condition that affects social interaction) differed in only one respect: an area of the brain that is part of the mirror neuron system showed lower activity rates in children with autism.

Now, children aren't monkeys, but the implication for learning in humans is significant. Neurologically speaking, learning occurs through the establishment of pathways that connect parts of the brain. These pathways are strengthened through repetition and use. The analogy of a path through a field of tall grass is helpful here. When no path yet exists, the initial journey is slow and inefficient; however, as the path gets more use, the grass lies down, and the trail is clearer. Think of the initial activation of brain pathways as a bird's-eye view of the untrampled field: It gives the learner a preliminary trail to follow and provides a rehearsal effect that causes the pathway to run more smoothly. This is where automaticity and fluency come in—not just in reading but for any complex task, such as the cognitive and social language demands inherent in group work.

Ongoing research in mirror neuron systems could also have profound implications for language development. If we are wired to learn vicariously by observing facial expressions and physical gestures, and then reflexively imitating those actions as a first step to language and appropriate social responses, then our face-to-face interactions with students take on even greater importance. The existence of mirror neural networks that govern the social aspects of language—such as gesture, body position, and facial expression—support the use of modeling and observation, particularly when assisting students who have difficulty relating well to others. In one promising study, children with autism were successfully taught about social language using video modeling of positive social language use (Sansoti & Powell-Smith, 2008).

Understanding the neuronal basis of language and learning serves as confirmation and further explication of research findings in the behavioral studies of education. Led by Vygotsky's (1978) theory of peer-mediated learning, a host of face-to-face instructional routines such as quickwrites, partner discussions, and role-playing and simulation activities have been designed to foster personal and academic growth.

Teachers Must Show, Not Tell

With mirroring in mind, it's important to focus on how to model the behaviors necessary to make group interactions effective and productive. For example, in order for students to become proficient at giving suggestions or providing explanations within their group, they need to be shown what those behaviors look like. If the teacher's modeling leans more toward "telling" students the appropriate behaviors versus "showing" them what those behaviors look and sound like, students are unlikely to make the leap from what their teacher does to what they are supposed to do in the group.

Webb, Nemer, and Ing (2006) studied the connection between the types of inter-actions used by teachers in middle school mathematics classrooms and those that occurred among students working in small groups. They discovered that although the teachers emphasized group norms (no put-downs, listening to others) and class-building activities to foster collaboration, students rarely offered specific help to one another because it was rarely exhibited by their teachers. Instead, the "help" they offered typically came in the form of telling a fellow student the answer without any explana-tion of how to arrive at it. In other words, students mimicked what their teacher had modeled, not what the teacher had intended for them to do. The researchers noted that "changing student behavior in the classroom without a concomitant focus on changing teachers' accustomed style and content of instruction" resulted in students who "seemed to utilize the skills they perfected in a didactic learning environment in the collaborative environment without much modification" (p. 108).

The danger of such small-group interactions is that the collaborative learning and consolidation of knowledge that group work is supposed to support will not occur in these circumstances. If group members who do not understand a concept are simply told the answer, they are more likely to believe that having the answer or completing the task is more important than the process of finding an answer or understanding the concept. The telling-not-helping interaction could also reinforce the kind of negative experiences that inhibit learning—particularly negative self-talk. Learners may remind themselves that they are "too stupid" to complete the task and can do so only when others give them the answers.

These subtleties in interaction can be difficult to quantify, and listening for them takes a practiced ear. We have found it useful in our own classrooms to teach the language of learning to our students so they may use it during their discussions with one another. We post the list of the types of language they can use with one another to foster a higher level of academic language (see Figure 3.2). Their ability to instruct one another, ask questions, make decisions, and so on represents the cognitive topography of learning acquisition.

Theresa Blank, a kindergarten teacher at North Oakview Elementary in Michi-gan, is well attuned to the language of learning. When she hears A. J. say to Violet, "Hey, Violet, maybe you should write that down!" Ms. Blank knows that A. J. is engaging in instructive discourse. When Garrett asks Jalen, "What other characters

Figure 3.2	Language of Learning Poster	
Language Objective	**What Is It?**	**What Does It Sound Like?**
To instruct	Giving directions	• "The first step is . . ." • "Next . . ." • "The last part is . . ."
To inquire	Asking questions	• "Who? What? When? Where? Why? How?" • "What do you think?"
To test	Deciding if something makes sense	• "I still have a question about . . ." • "What I learned is . . ."
To describe	Telling about something	• Use descriptive words and details.
To compare and contrast	Showing how two things are alike and different	• "Here is something they both have in common . . ." • "These are different from each other because . . ."
To explain	Giving examples	• "This is an example of . . ." • "This is important because . . ."
To analyze	Discussing the parts of a bigger idea	• "The parts of this include . . ." • "We can make a diagram of this."
To hypothesize	Making a prediction based on what is known	• "I can predict that . . ." • "I believe that ___ will happen because . . ." • "What might happen if . . ."
To deduce	Drawing a conclusion or arriving at an answer	• "The answer is ___ because . . ."
To evaluate	Judging something	• "I agree with this because . . ." • "I disagree because . . ." • "I recommend that . . ." • "A better solution would be . . ." • "The factors that are most important are . . ."

were in the book?" she recognizes that they are using the language of inquiry. Learning doesn't stop there, and we want them to be conscious of the ways in which they analyze, formulate explanations, and evaluate ideas. When Garrett reaffirms Jalen's idea by saying, "Oh, yeah, you're right!" he is demonstrating a 5-year-old's nascent ability to evaluate. Although they are years away from recognizing it themselves, Ms. Blank notices how her students are constructing meaning together.

Instructional Routines That Foster Face-to-Face Interaction

Over the years, a host of face-to-face instructional routines have been designed to foster productive interaction in student group work. We will look at three we've found to be particularly useful: quickwrites, partner discussions, and role playing. Our examples start with individual work and move to partner and then group interaction, and we'll show how this progression of routines builds confidence and stamina for interactive learning.

Quickwrites

It may seem odd that we begin a discussion of interactive routines with an independent activity, but we view quickwrites as an important gateway to meaningful interaction. These brief writing events, typically one to five minutes in length, provide learners with time to collect their thoughts and formalize their ideas before they engage in a discussion with another student. Having writing to refer to can also provide a bridge over the awkward pauses that shy or reluctant students may experience as they struggle to get a conversation going. For many students, quickwrites represent a starting point for the meaningful exchange of ideas.

The writing prompt for a quickwrite can be tailored specifically to the content being taught ("How would you explain cell division to your younger brother?") or it can be more general. Here are some of our favorites:

- What's the best thing you learned today?

- What was confusing to you in today's lesson?

- What do you already know about this topic?

- How did you help yourself to learn today?

- Crystal ball: What do you think you will learn about tomorrow?

• Yesterday's news: What does a person who was absent yesterday need to know about the lesson?

• Finish this thought: I was proud of myself today when I . . .

• What are the five best habits to have to be successful in this class?

• My goals for this week are . . .

• In the next 60 seconds, write down all the words you think of when you hear about _____.

• When I read about _____, I was confused because _____.

Quickwrite prompts can be used before, during, and after a lesson. These brief writing interludes allow students to create a chain of evidence of their own thinking and learning. For example, during a lesson about the progressive activist Upton Sinclair, Spenser was given a quickwrite prompt related to a reading about persistence. He wrote the following paragraph in response:

> [Persistence] connects to Upton Sinclair's plight for safe food and safe work conditions. He had to spend seven weeks working as a laborer to gather evidence. Then, after trying to publish his article, he had to go against Ogden Armour. He won this, and put out his article. However, the public did not react to the part about the laborers' conditions as he wanted. Then, as he wrote more articles about laborer conditions, the president told him to stop. However, he persisted and got healthier foods and better worker conditions.

After completing this quickwrite, Spenser was ready and able to share his thinking during a partner discussion.

Partner Discussions

Telling students to "turn to your partner and . . ." is common in the lexicon of teachers, but we find that, too often, there is little follow-up determining the nature of the partners' conversation and whether it was actually productive. Having students complete a quickwrite before partner interaction increases the likelihood that these conversations are productive because the activity provides both a catalyst and a focus for the conversation.

Once students begin to discuss their thoughts with a partner, teachers need to leap into action as well. This isn't the time to reshuffle materials or prepare for the next part of the lesson; it is a golden opportunity to gain insight into what students do and don't understand at a given moment in time. Nancy keeps a few transparencies on a clipboard for such occasions and circulates among groups to write down what she hears. For example, after students in Spenser's class completed their quickwrites about persistence, they were asked to discuss them with a partner. Nancy listened in as Spenser and Josh talked about Upton Sinclair:

> *Spenser:* I can see why [Sinclair] got frustrated with the people who read his book. He wanted them to think about the workers.
>
> *Josh:* Right. I wrote down that quote about "aiming for their heart and hitting them in the stomach."
>
> *Spenser:* He didn't give up, though. Like that little ant in the story. There's an obstacle, like a lawsuit or whatever, and he wouldn't stop.
>
> *Josh:* My bulldog is like that! She never gets tired of pulling on her rope toy.

Nancy wrote down "persistence like a bulldog" and moved on to the next group. After collecting a few more quotes, she displayed the transparency on the overhead projector and discussed each quote with the whole class. In some cases, students joined in to elaborate, while in other cases, they did not. Nancy likes using this technique to move partner discussions to the larger class so that they can hear ideas from other groups. It also adds a measure of accountability to the mix when they see her coming with the clipboard!

Role Playing and Simulations

Students enjoy role playing and often can recall participating in a scenario long after their schooling is over. Doug recalls playing a stock market investment game in his 11th grade U.S. history class. His team was given "$100" to invest in a combination of growth and investment stocks. Many years later, Doug is proud to say that his team converted their original investment into a return of $221. Other popular simulations include baseball math, virtual dissections, and putting a literary character on trial. One of Nancy and Doug's favorite mock trials was when

Goldilocks was put on trial in Aida Allen's kindergarten class for breaking and entering. (The verdict? Guilty as charged!)

Physical activities in which students simulate a process or idea can also create interaction and interdependence and build conceptual and factual knowledge that is otherwise more challenging to learn independently. For example, we have watched our colleague Maria Grant teach her earth science students about the action of P-waves and S-waves in earthquakes by asking them to line up next to one another and place their outstretched arms over the shoulders of the people on either side of them (think of the Rockettes in a chorus line). She gently pushes the student at the beginning of the line, triggering a P-wave as each student sways and then stands up straight again. To contrast this movement with an S-wave, Ms. Grant then asks the first person in the line to bend forward at the waist and stand up again. The action of the first student causes each successive person to repeat the same motion, making a ripple down the line. In these group interactions, students are literally experiencing both wave patterns and physically confronting why P-waves move more quickly than S-waves.

After this whole-class simulation, Ms. Grant gives groups of four students a Slinky and a length of rope and asks them to determine which item best portrays each type of wave. As they solve the problem, the student groups use their common experience of "being waves" to support their discussions and consolidate their understanding of these complex concepts. (For the record, a Slinky stretched out and back is best for demonstrating a P-wave, while a rope that is whipped up and down provides a great representation of the S-wave's perpendicular shear motion.)

Inside Three Classrooms

Let's peek inside our three example classrooms and see how the teachers are incorporating and supporting face-to-face interaction. Look for examples of starting small with partner group work and of supportive routines for interaction, such as prompts, quickwrites, and role playing.

Ms. Allen, Elementary School Language Arts

Aida Allen uses what is called a *whip-around* routine to facilitate the sharing of ideas between partners and the whole class. To initiate a whip-around, she poses questions to partner groups and asks them to respond with a list of ideas. For example, her 4th grade students, all English learners, have been mastering common prefixes and suffixes. She asks them first to brainstorm individually all the words they can think of that start with the prefix *pre*. For the next minute, each student composes a list. Then she asks them to turn to their partner and combine their lists into a single one with no duplicate words. Next, Ms. Allen invites all students to stand, and going around the room by partners, each partner reads one word from their list. Other groups cross off those words that have been read. As students read off words such as *prepare, prevent,* and *pretend,* partners eliminate these from their lists. When their list is exhausted, partners sit down. In a matter of three minutes or so, every student has participated, and the class has composed an extensive list of words.

Ms. Vogel, Middle School Humanities

In Kathy Vogel's 7th grade class, partners continued work on simulating a Larry King interview. After modeling and analyzing a real interview, Ms. Vogel asked the partners to select a fictional or real character who could explain an economic, social, or political problem of a nation in the eastern hemisphere. She distributed a list of prompts to support the partners' brainstorming about interview content and instructed students to "use your knowledge of the countries we have studied to decide what you will focus on." She added, "You'll use this list to propose an interview to me." The list contained the following prompts:

- The country we are selecting is _____.

- The person, event, or issue we have selected is _____.

- Important contributions the subject made in the field of _____.

- How the subject became interested in _____.

- The subject's childhood.

- How the subject dealt with changes and adversity.

- What influences the subject had in his/her life.

- How the subject would like to be remembered.

- What the subject might say to people in present time.

- What steps led up to this event?

- How the issue affected the world.

- What is the issue's lasting significance?

- What can we learn from this issue?

Ms. Vogel told us that this list seemed to increase students' motivation and focus their research as they composed their scripts.

The role playing also required a lot of face-to-face interaction as groups rehearsed and tried to add authenticity to the interviews. For guidance, they consulted a rubric they had made with Ms. Vogel, which laid out performance criteria. The interviewers wore Larry King's trademark suspenders and glasses and sat behind a desk decorated to look like the one on the real set of *Larry King Live*.

Mr. Gibbs, High School Social Studies

Like most classrooms, Brian Gibbs's has students with a wide range of academic, language, and social skills. To ensure that all students have an opportunity to contribute to discussions and share what they know, Mr. Gibbs uses a variety of routines and protocols to level the communication playing field. For example, he implements and enforces "wait time" to help temper the impetuous students who can't help but blurt out the answers (sometimes before the question has even been posed) and to provide reticent or reflective students time to process the question. Wait time can be particularly important to English language learners and students with auditory processing challenges, who are at a distinct disadvantage in responding quickly to questions and participating in discussions.

Another interaction-promoting routine that Mr. Gibbs uses regularly is a variation on a cooperative structure designed by Spencer Kagan (1994). It is called "Head-to-Head Write Off" and lends itself particularly well to controversial topics. Students are paired off and move their desks together in a head-to-head arrangement, as if they are prepared to arm wrestle. Mr. Gibbs, after assigning a topic (say, the analysis of a historical figure), poses a question such as, "Does your historical character think that forcible integration would be good for our high school?" Students consider the question and respond to it in writing for two full minutes. When time is called, partners exchange papers and have two minutes to read what their partner has written and respond to it in writing (no talking). The exchange is repeated, creating a back-and-forth written dialogue (sometimes *argument,* depending on the writers' viewpoints). The number of exchanges can vary depending on the topic's level of controversy and complexity. Following the final exchange, partners are given up to five minutes to talk about their responses and clarify their opinions. At this point, partners are often bursting at the seams to talk.

Next, Mr. Gibbs typically guides the entire class in a discussion of their Head-to-Head Write Offs. In the early stages of group work, these discussions are highly structured, with Mr. Gibbs directing the type of information to be shared as well as providing a reporting prompt (e.g., "One thing Laura and I agreed on was . . . and one thing we disagreed about was . . ."). As students demonstrate skills such as sharing airtime, expressing opinions, soliciting responses, or holding the floor, the structure of the discussion can be less teacher directed. A clear benefit of write-off exchanges is more thoughtful, rigorous, and substantial discussions.

4

Ensuring Individual
and Group Accountability

All for one and one for all. This is the code that bonds D'Artagnan and his compatriots. But the Musketeers' motto is about more than their honor; it expresses their understanding that the group draws its strength from the success of its individual members. Each is at once accountable to himself *and* to his fellow Musketeers.

Accountability has acquired a somewhat negative connotation in the past decade. In some circles, the word is now associated with sanctions; in fact, *accountability* is synonymous with *responsibility*. This is the meaning we have in mind for this chapter's exploration of individual and group accountability. Just as Dumas's Musketeers held themselves accountable to one another, each member of a productive work group shares a sense of responsibility to the other members.

Two levels of accountability should be built into any productive group work: individual accountability and group accountability. Each individual must be responsible for his or her contribution to the joint task: *Did I do* what *I was supposed to do,* as well *as I was supposed to do it, and* when *I was supposed to do it?* At the same time, all group members collectively must also be responsible for how well they accomplished the overall task: *Did we do* what *we were supposed to do,* as well *as we were supposed to do it, and* when *we were supposed to do it?* Regardless of the rigor or duration of the collaborative learning task, each student needs to clearly understand his or her individual role as well as what the group is expected to produce or accomplish. Students also need to know how they will be assessed and need to receive feedback for both levels of work.

Building Accountability into the Task

We've all heard the criticisms of group work—one person gets stuck doing most of the work, or fast-moving groups leave members behind in their rush to complete the task. But the question these criticisms raise is a good one: How *do* you make sure that all the members are doing their fair share? Our answer is that collaboration and interdependence must be built into group tasks. However, a group project that requires that all individuals learn and contribute requires an accountability system capable of monitoring the learning processes used by the group and its individual members.

Barron and colleagues (1998) researched the use of problem- and project-based learning in classrooms and found that certain factors were present in the design of the most successful. Using these factors and adding a few recommendations of our own, we offer these guidelines for ensuring accountability in group work:

1. Design tasks that emphasize larger learning goals ("How to make healthy food choices") rather than discrete knowledge ("What the food pyramid looks like"). This makes the division of labor into an assembly-line production unlikely.

2. Give students experience with small tasks before asking them to tackle longer projects. An incremental start helps them build the stamina required to sustain work extending over several days or weeks and gives individuals the practice needed to be successful in the group.

3. Establish timelines for both individual and group completion of each phase of the assignment.

4. Create interim steps for discussing individual and group progress and providing feedback.

5. Ask students to evaluate themselves and their group's efforts. We have groups complete their evaluation on one form so that all members see each other's words. It's amazing how honest they are about what they did and did not do.

6. Factor in both individual and group evaluations when grading the assignment. This means that each member receives two grades for the assignment—an individual grade and a group grade.

Let's see how one teacher incorporated some of the guidelines in a shorter group work task. Third grade teacher Jamie Wilcox, from North Oakview Elementary in Michigan, taught a unit on economics in her social studies class. Her goal was to help students learn about the effects of scarcity and opportunity cost, and how to analyze the kinds of human, natural, and capital resources available in a given situation. To show how scarcity influences choice, she modeled the use of a decision tree graphic organizer to chart what the characters in Pat Hutchins's book *The Doorbell Rang* did as new people kept showing up to get chocolate chip cookies. This prepared her students to use the same decision tree graphic organizer with a different story.

Then, Ms. Wilcox developed a group task to give her students the opportunity to consolidate their understanding with their peers. Using Margaree King Mitchell's *Uncle Jed's Barbershop* and Dr. Seuss's *The Lorax,* students created a decision tree to describe the choices the main characters make during the course of the stories. The task was more complex than merely recounting the plot. Students were asked to evaluate the choices in order to figure out what was gained and what was given up as a result of each decision.

Ms. Wilcox used assigned roles to ensure fair work distribution. Each group consisted of a discussion leader, a reader, a recorder, and a reporter. She spent time with each group during the task and looked for evidence that the roles were being carried out effectively. Because students had learned these roles earlier in the school year, they were familiar with the requirements for each and could concentrate on the cognitive aspects of the task. However, Ms. Wilcox also provided table tents that described each role, and she referred to these when a student needed redirection.

Every member of the group also made an individual evaluation of the characters' decisions, deciding whether the opportunity costs were too high or not and justifying their opinions with evidence. In this way, Ms. Wilcox constructed a collaborative learning task that focused on learning larger concepts, and students completed both a group assignment (the decision tree) and an individual one (the evaluation of the character's decision making).

Setting Expectations

To be accountable, students must understand the expectations for their learning as individuals and as group members. These expectations should include both what they are to contribute and how. Remember, although productive group work leads to a useful outcome or end result, it isn't only about completing a task; it's about the process—how learning occurs.

There are a number of useful tools that can help ensure students understand what's expected from them. Timelines can establish what group members must accomplish and when. Checklists can outline the steps required for completing a task, like a collaborative poster or writing a readers' theater version of a text. And group members can use checklists to monitor their individual and group progress toward task completion. Finally, rubrics are a way to establish criteria for grading and relieve the teacher of having to subjectively evaluate work. Our experience suggests that students should be involved in establishing criteria for the rubric. Participation leads to better understanding of the criteria and how they relate to the task goal, and it can focus students' performance on achieving the expected outcome. (Rubistar is a free Web site where teachers can create and share rubrics. Find it at www.rubistar.4teachers.org.)

Note, too, that both checklists and rubrics can help guide students in the hows and how-wells of productive group work: participation, interaction, and the group skills of listening and providing helpful feedback.

Giving Feedback

Feedback lies at the center of accountability. The teacher's role in fostering individual and group accountability is to create assessment systems that encourage feedback among the members of the group *and* between the teacher and student. This feedback should be instructive—not designed as a "gotcha" to determine who's slacking off. At first blush this may seem simple, but providing this support for group learning can challenge some teachers' philosophies about grading, particularly when evaluation supplants formative assessment. However, if we don't make the effort to help students to assess their work and determine the next step to take, they will confuse learning with getting it right the first time. As Brookhart (2008) puts it, "If part of the classroom culture is to 'always get things right,' then if something needs improvement, it's 'wrong'" (p. 2).

An accountability system that evaluates progress in learning—not just getting an answer right or completing a task—requires that the learning process be monitored and students receive feedback during the group work as well as at the end of the assignment. This monitoring should cover individual contributions to the group and the group work as a whole. It can be done by the teacher, the group itself, or both. We'll discuss specific approaches for peer feedback in Chapter 5 and examine group self-assessment in Chapter 6. For now, we'll look at two ways to promote individual and group accountability between teacher and student: observation and conferencing.

Observation

Teachers have a range of options for assessing individual group members and groups as a whole but frequently identify observations as the most important source of information about students (West, 1998). Yetta Goodman (1985) coined the term "kidwatching" to describe how astute teachers collect information about student performance. Recording kidwatching observations can be as simple as using a clipboard with sticky notes in order to jot quick comments about a student's participation in group work. We find it useful to use an anecdotal record form with the name of the student, date, duration of observation, and description of the observed task (see Figure 4.1). These data can be helpful when later analyzing the information gathered over several observations.

Checklists are another option for recording observations. They allow teachers to specify particular dimensions for observations and provide a means of summarizing. For example, a teacher can prepare a checklist for monitoring a group text or book club discussion that covers students' preparation, group behavior, and connections made. The list can reveal strategies used by students to make meaning of the text and whether students are making connections between their comments and the comments of their peers (see Figure 4.2).

Conferencing

Time is a teacher's most precious commodity, and finding opportunities to conference with students can be difficult. Even so, setting aside time to talk with students can give teachers information they might not gain otherwise. Conferences may be informal and relatively short (just a few minutes) or longer. They may

Figure 4.1	Anecdotal Observation Record Form

Name of Student: _____   Begin Time: _____

Date: _____   End Time: _____

Group Arrangement:

Individual: _____
Partner: _____
Small Group: _____
Whole Class: _____

Description of Observed Task:

Observations:

be with individuals, partners, or groups. Students' timelines, checklists, and rubrics can be helpful in conference discussions of progress, or a teacher may use a structured script of questions to engage learners about their work. Whatever the format, the goal of conferencing is for the teacher not only to gather information but also to promote the students' own ability to assess and reflect on their learning.

Figure 4.2	Book Club Checklist

Name of Student: _____   Date: _____

Discussion Text: _____

Book Club Discussion Behaviors	Not in Evidence	Emerging	In Use
Preparation:			
Has read selection prior to group discussion			
Has written in response journal			
Has noted unfamiliar words or phrases			
Group Behaviors:			
Asks other group members questions about the text			
Extends other students' responses			
Respects the opinions of others			
Connections:			
Makes connections between text and self			
Makes connection between focus text and other readings			
Makes connections between text and other students' responses			
Other Notes:			

The Neural Basis for Individual and Group Accountability

Productive group work that promotes accountability and feedback shapes learning. We see evidence of this in our students' thinking and products, but thanks to neuroimaging techniques, we can confirm this shaping at a biological level. The brain actually changes as a result of learning, a phenomenon called neuroplasticity.

Myths about the brain tend to persist despite research that provides evidence refuting them; the "Mozart effect" of music on intelligence is one well-known example. A most stubborn myth to dispel has been that brains cannot change after critical periods of development that occur early in life. Although it is true that behavior patterns sometimes remain rigid, neuroscience research has confirmed that the neural connections in the brain are continually reshaped by experiences. This plasticity is especially pronounced in the amygdalae (LeDoux, 2002). You'll recall from Chapter 2 that these structures are important for attention and processing emotions. Indeed, it appears that the attention system regulates the plasticity of the brain and that sustained attention to a task or skill is associated with changes at the neuronal level. Conversely, stress is negatively associated with attention (McEwen, 2006). When attention is paired with reward, these changes occur even faster (Doidge, 2007). Feedback plays an important role in focusing a student's attention, encouraging practice, and providing a reward for both.

To explain the concept of neuroplasticity, it is helpful to compare it to a practice often used by architects. Rather than laying down paths and sidewalks between buildings according to a prescribed set of rules, sometimes architects will allow the users to determine where these features should go. By simply observing the natural footpaths that emerge after a few weeks of use, the best routes become apparent. These paths are then paved and made more permanent, becoming even easier and faster to traverse. The creation of pathways in the brain follows a similar pattern. When a person attempts a task, a nascent network appears. Through sustained attention, corrective feedback, and repetition, these pathways become stronger. Indeed, a maxim in neuroscience is that "neurons that fire together, wire together," as synaptic and cell connectivity strengthens through association (Hebb, 1949). Over time, the brain "paves" these neural paths with myelin, allowing the signals to move more rapidly. When students engage in group work that offers them feedback and holds them accountable for their learning, they are paving these pathways.

Instructional Routines That Ensure Individual and Group Accountability

Let's look now at four instructional routines that provide individual and group accountability and help ensure a group's work is truly productive for all its members.

Numbered Heads Together

This grouping strategy, designed by Spencer Kagan (1994), is an excellent example of the task structure fostering an accountability system that takes each member's learning into consideration. In numbered heads, students are grouped into teams of four, and each member is assigned a number. The teacher then poses a question to the groups, who discuss the answer among themselves. Group members are motivated to make sure that each person understands the answer because it is unknown who will be required to supply it. After time for discussion, the teacher announces which number will respond. For example, if the teacher calls for number three, the student in the group assigned number three must be the one to answer in writing on paper or a response board. This approach works well for every content area and is especially appropriate for reviewing concepts.

During a review of the rock cycle in a 7th grade classroom, Ms. Andrews posed a question about which rocks are part of the cycle and which are not. In discussing the question, each of the groups had the opportunity to review what they knew, expand their understanding of the content, and provide feedback to one another. An excerpt from their discussion follows:

> *Onisha:* I know that sedimentary rocks are part of the rock cycle because they are just broken off parts of other rocks.
>
> *Kahlid:* Yeah, so the bigger rocks have to be part of the cycle too.
>
> *Dakota:* But sedimentary isn't just the broken part of big rocks. Ms. Andrews also said that they can be chemical, like crystals.
>
> *Onisha:* I have a crystal at home that is purple. My dad told me that crystals grow like they're almost alive. So they have to be part of the rock cycle.
>
> *Jasmine:* I think that crystals are part of the rock cycle because they are examples of sedimentary rocks. I think that all rocks are part of

the cycle because the book [Bailey and Lilly's *The Rock Factory: A Story About the Rock Cycle*] told us that rocks are recycled.

Kahlid: Yeah, I agree. That means that rocks are always changing.

Onisha: But it's slow. It takes a long time for them to change. Like, I'll be dead when most of these rocks are changed.

Dakota: But I think that the rock cycle is for Earth. I think that "meteorites" is the answer to the question about rocks that don't change.

Kahlid: Oh, yeah, I remember Ms. Andrews saying that.

Onisha: I forgot. You're on it today.

Jasmine: Meteorites are the ones that scientists are still questioning. I think we should answer that Earth rocks are *all* part of the rock cycle and that meteorites are special; some are part of the cycle and some might not be.

As students held their discussions in advance of the whole-group responses, Ms. Andrews spent time observing one group for each question. She tallied the number of times each student spoke during the discussion and further noted when clarifying questions were asked and answered. These sampled observations gave her a sense of the relative rates of participation within each group.

When Ms. Andrews called the number four, Onisha was the student required to respond for her group. Essentially, she answered as Jasmine and Dakota had suggested. Ms. Andrews was very pleased with this thoughtful response. She had only briefly noted the issue of meteorites and had expected that students would focus on the all-inclusive nature of the rock cycle.

Collaboratively Constructed Products

Although group tasks that culminate in a single product can lead to unequal distribution of the workload, such as one member doing most of the work, there are times when a single product is necessary. Think of an informational poster, for instance, or a PowerPoint presentation, or a group writing task. When this is the case, building in individual accountability measures can prevent problems.

For an informational poster, teachers can require each member of the group to use a different-colored ink to write their contributions and then ask students to sign the poster in their assigned color. This way each student's contribution is evident to the group, the individual, and the teacher. To ensure that group members are familiar with the content developed by their groupmates, teachers can require that each member develop two or three multiple-choice items for his or her section. Groupmates must teach the details of their portion to one another, and then all are accountable for a composite quiz. We often garner representative questions for a class quiz on all presentations of collaborative projects, which further encourages students to take notes and listen attentively.

Progressive Writing

During a progressive dinner, a group travels to each member's house to eat a different course of a meal. Progressive writing works in much the same way. Each member of the group begins writing a paper and continues for a fixed period of time (usually five minutes) before passing his or her paper to another member of the group (say, the person sitting to the right). Each group member reads what the person before has written and then continues the writing. This pattern is repeated until every member has written a portion of each paper. Then, the group members discuss the contents of all the papers they've written and nominate the best representative paper for submission (Frey & Fisher, 2005).

Figure 4.3 contains a sample progressive writing paper on the topic of the French Revolution from a 10th grade classroom. About halfway through the unit of study, students were asked to complete this task as part of their productive group work. The teacher used the papers to address misconceptions and target individual students for reteaching.

Writing Frames

We often use writing frames in group work. They serve both as an effective scaffold for using academic language and as evidence of individual group members' learning and contributions during group work.

When we first heard about writing frames, we have to admit that we were a bit worried that they would be a crutch for students and would encourage dull formulaic writing. But our experience and research suggest otherwise (Fisher & Frey, 2003), and we were pleased to learn that these frames are even recommended

Figure 4.3	Group Progressive Writing Sample

The French Revolution was the most bloody and violent of the three major revolutions. The French Revolution was focused on an unfair distribution of power between the first two estates and the ~~because~~ third estate. The first estate was the clergy men and the second was the nobles; both were not taxed at all and held very little of the population. The third estate included everyone else and were taxed. The third estate didn't like being ~~treated~~ unfairly so they decided to make a change. They had meetings for change and the king didn't like that. The people revolted by storming the Bastille, an armory and prison which represented all the corruption of France and the inequality. The women also revolted by marching to Versailles ~~alled~~ to bring back the King and the Queen back to ~~Versailles~~ Paris. Before, the third estate rallied together and created the Tennis court Oath, declaring that they would stand together until their own Constitution was passed. The third estate was also called the National Assembly. This group established the Tennis court oath because the king tried to stop any and all of their progress.

in college composition classes, on the grounds that "even the most creative forms of expression depend on established patterns and structures, [and] creativity and originality lie not in the avoidance of established forms, but in the imaginative use of them" (Graff & Birkenstein, 2006, pp. 10–11).

We've seen writing frames used in group work across the curriculum and across grade levels. For example, Ms. Aracelli, a 2nd grade teacher, asked student groups to use a writing frame to practice asking and answering questions using past tense verbs. The question and response read:

> What did your (family member type) _____ do on _____?
> My (family member type) _____ (verb) _____ and _____ on _____.

In their productive work groups, students in Ms. Aracelli's class talked about Thanksgiving and then asked and answered questions of each other. They used verbs from the word wall and identified family members from their journals. Jasmine wrote: *What did your dad do on Thanksgiving?* James responded: *My dad ate turkey and ham and watched TV on Thanksgiving.* Mirah responded: *My aunt ate apple pie and pumpkin pie on Thanksgiving.* Ms. Aracelli listened in as students talked with one another, ensuring both individual and group accountability.

Ninth grade English teacher Kelly Moore used the following paragraph frame in group work to help readers understand the mood of a book:

> In the story, _____, the author creates a mood of _____. One of the ways he/she makes us feel _____ is by _____. Another way he/she creates this mood is by _____. For example, _____ _____. Most important, the mood of _____ makes the reader feel _____ _____. As the story progresses, the characters in _____ learn to _____. As we read the story we learn to _____ also.

To model the use of the frame, Ms. Moore chose to focus on E. B. White's *Charlotte's Web,* a book that most of her 9th grade students knew. She then asked students to use the frame to write individually about the mood of the book they were reading in their group. A group reading Stephenie Meyer's *Twilight* talked about the mood of the book, and then each member used the frame to construct his or her own paragraph. One student's paragraph is shown in Figure 4.4. Group members read one another's responses and then had a conversation about the similarities and differences between their paragraphs. Afterward, Ms. Moore used the paragraphs to assess student understanding and to plan guided, small-group instruction based on the needs identified in the papers.

Writing frames may also be used across content areas. For example, chemistry and physics teacher Ms. Grant regularly has students use frames to summarize

Figure 4.4	Student Writing Sample Using a Mood Frame

Susana Jimenez
November 17, 2008

MOOd

In the book, Twilight, the author creates a mood of fascination and wonder. One of the ways she makes us feel fascination is by talking about the forever living vampires. Another way she creates this mood is by adding super powers and speed to the amazing vampires. For example, Edward can read people's mind and Alice can see the feature. Most important, the mood of wonder makes the reader feel likes there's so much more to ordinary people because you never know who might have a little extra to them. As the story progresses, the characters in Twilight learn to adapt to the living in forks. As we read the story we learn to keep a sense of wonder as well.

understanding as part of their productive group work during labs. In a lab on wave motion, she provided students with the following starter:

> In summary, _____ has the property of _____. Our evidence includes _____, _____, and _____. Thus, it seems reasonable to suggest _____.

Inside Three Classrooms

Throughout this chapter, we've discussed the importance of designing productive group work that includes accountability and providing opportunities for students to receive feedback about their individual and group work. We have also illustrated different instructional routines that promote a fair division of labor to ensure all students are actively engaged in learning by doing (and not by watching their peers work). Let's turn now to the classrooms of our three teachers to see how they design productive group tasks with individual and group accountability.

Ms. Allen, Elementary School Science

Aida Allen's 2nd grade students were studying nutrition in their science class. They had learned about the U.S. Department of Agriculture's food pyramid and its recommendations regarding the daily number of servings of grains, fruits, vegetables, beans and meat, and dairy products. They had studied the food pyramid poster displayed in their classroom and learned to accurately categorize common foods. Ms. Allen had modeled how she makes choices about foods, and students had analyzed the school's lunch menu for a week, noting which items were lacking or represented too frequently. With this foundation laid, Ms. Allen felt her students were ready to tackle the group work task she had designed for the unit. The first step was for each student to keep a food diary for a day using a worksheet designed by the USDA.

The next day, Ms. Allen assigned students to groups of four and asked them to develop a collaborative poster using the food pyramid and the information in their food diaries. Each student used a different-colored marker to enter data on the poster. For instance, Beto told his groupmates that he had spaghetti and meatballs with a salad the evening before. Leo and Mariana agreed that this meal contained meat, vegetables, and fruit, but they weren't quite sure which group the pasta belonged to. Adriana used the food pyramid poster to confirm that pasta was a grain and showed her groupmates why that answer was correct. The process repeated as each member read from his or her food diary and wrote the information on the poster. At the bottom of the poster, they wrote about their collective choices and set a goal for tomorrow's meals. At the end of the task, the group turned in their collaborative poster and the food diaries of each member, ensuring that Ms. Allen would have both group and individual measures to assess their progress.

Ms. Vogel, Middle School Humanities

We have seen how Kathy Vogel modeled an interview with an influential person and distributed a list of prompts to facilitate students' efforts to create interview questions. Next, she went on to hold conferences with each team to discuss the partners' progress and assist them in locating the necessary source information to present a fully realized proposal.

For their *Larry King Live* interview, Dave and Eric chose to create a fictional Israeli government official with conflicted feelings about the protracted Arab–Israeli conflict. As Ms. Vogel conferred with them, she noted the contributions each of them had made as they collected information about the historical roots of the conflict, the creation of Israel in 1948, and Yitzhak Rabin's assassination in 1995. The boys met with her several times over the next week as they added information to their proposal, which was evolving into an outline for their interview script. By consulting with students during this weeklong project, Ms. Vogel was able to gather information about the progress of individual students as well as monitor the progress of the teams as they prepared for their interviews.

Mr. Gibbs, High School World History

Students in Brian Gibbs's 10th grade world history class were finishing a unit on Rome built around the theme "Choices and Responsibilities: The Forces That Shape Society." They had just completed a mock trial in which Julius Caesar was put on trial for destroying the Roman Republic. As observers or actors in the trial, students examined the choices made by the various characters and drew inferences as to their motives and beliefs about duty, leadership, and society. Because the earliest version of a newspaper was the Roman *Acta Diurna,* first posted in 59 BCE on the orders of Julius Caesar, it is fitting that the culminating activity for this unit was a special edition of that paper focused on Caesar's trial.

Mr. Gibbs placed students into groups of four and explained that each group would be responsible for producing a newspaper containing five articles illustrating the multiple perspectives elicited in the trial and how these perspectives connected to the unit's theme. Students received specific instructions on what to include: (1) an informative piece giving a factual account of the trial; (2) interviews with two different key players in the trial; (3) a personal editorial or commentary focused on the trial; and (4) an advice column responding to a request by Portia about how to handle her husband Brutus's dark mood and refusal to share what is troubling him. Earlier in the year, students learned how to write different types of articles typically found in a newspaper. This was an opportunity to apply those skills in a new context.

To ensure that all students were actively involved in learning, Mr. Gibbs built a number of individual and group accountability metrics into the activity. Each day he assigned one of the articles for homework. Students knew they would be sharing their draft articles in class the next day and that they would receive an individual grade for each of the five articles. Both these measures increased the level of individual accountability. In class, students shared and discussed each other's articles. They underlined powerful phrases and vocabulary in each other's work, checking for accuracy and evaluating how well the ideas or evidence used in the article connected to the unit's theme. The group then worked collaboratively, culling the best ideas from the individual articles to produce a single article. Every team member had to sign off on the final article indicating that they agreed it represented their best thinking, before it could be published in their newspaper.

During the publication phase of the activity, students took on different roles or tasks (proofreader, copy editor, layout producer, graphic designer) and followed a production schedule with set deadlines. Each group received a team grade based on how well their newspaper met the criteria in an assessment rubric. Students also completed a peer assessment for each member of their group. These assessments included considerations such as doing assigned work on time, contributions made during face-to-face work time, and interacting with groupmates in productive ways. A student's final grade for the newspaper activity consisted of his or her individual scores for articles, the group's newspaper score, and the scores received on peer assessments. Mr. Gibbs combined the activity's score with scores from other unit activities, quizzes, and tests to determine each student's unit grade.

5

Building Interpersonal and Small-Group Skills

As Winnie-the-Pooh said, "You can't stay in your part of the forest waiting for others to come to you. You have to go to them sometimes."

We all have an innate desire to connect with others but sometimes feel unsure about how to do so. Teachers often see students suspended between wanting to interact and being afraid to attempt to. Just think of new students on their first day of school. They slide quietly into their desk, their eyes darting about looking for a friendly face in a room full of strangers. Their wary expressions relax as they catch a smile from a student across the room or when a classmate shows them where to find the water fountain. Some newcomers will hang back longer than others, but most make connections. These interactions in class, on the playground, and in the lunchroom turn into friendships. A few students will cause more concern as they struggle to engage or reach out, but with some mediation from a caring adult, these students, too, almost always find their allies.

Even when students know one another better, they can be hesitant about interacting, especially when they are asked to work together on an unfamiliar task. Students from kindergarten to high school are still in the process of forming an awareness of others and developing the social skills necessary for productive inter-action. That's where we, as teachers, can help. We can model social skills and provide opportunities to practice them, and we can create routines and group tasks that help students develop and expand their interpersonal skills. Often, the specific small-group skills needed for productive group work (a few of which are shown in Figure 5.1) must be taught and reinforced.

In our view, the skills of *thinking and communicating with clarity, active listening, giving peers feedback,* and *considering different perspectives* are particularly important for working productively in groups. It's part of a teacher's job to help students build the social muscles that are necessary to negotiate a complex world of differing cultures, languages, and values. We must make sure that students leave us comfortable and confident about connecting with others as they venture out of their part of the forest.

The Neural Basis of Interpersonal and Small-Group Skills

All interpersonal and small-group skills have a neurological basis. A particular area of the cortex, called the right temporoparietal junction (TPJ), appears to play an important part in social interaction, empathy, attention, and metacognition. This region is located above and just behind the right ear and serves as a critical meeting point for several important brain functions that flow into and out of the area. In particular, there is "speculation that the right TPJ is specialized for the possibly uniquely human ability to reason about others' affective and cognitive mental states" (Decety & Lamm, 2007, p. 581). In other words, this part of the brain may be responsible for our capacity to understand that someone else's thoughts and feelings are different from our own.

The ability to identify our thoughts and feelings as specific to us, and not as universal, has been described as *theory of mind.* With its attending empathetic and social skills, a theory of mind takes years to develop. When very young children "hide" by covering their eyes, they are showing that they think what *they* see is the same as what *you* see. Children are beginning to develop a theory of mind when they start to differentiate themselves from their mother; exhibit joint attention to an object, as when being read to; and point at something to direct another person's attention. Generally, at about 3 or 4 years of age, children demonstrate an understanding that others have a different view of the world from their own. And eventually, children develop the ability to infer another's intentions or motivations and predict their actions. An interesting hypothesis has been posed that people with autism may

Figure 5.1	Common Interpersonal Skills
Skill	**Operational Definition**
Leadership	• Offers guidance and organizational suggestions to help the group complete tasks • Allows others to voice opinions and assume responsibilities • Shares in successes and failures • Encourages the group to move toward their goal
Decision making	• Listens to the opinions of others and takes them into consideration • Identifies possible courses of action and accurately describes the costs and benefits of each • Is willing to make a choice when the group needs to come to a decision
Trust building	• Follows through on commitments to others • Contributes to a positive atmosphere • Disagrees respectfully • Accurately assesses his or her own competence
Turn taking	• Listens when others are talking and does not interrupt • Acknowledges others who have spoken • Makes sure all others are included • Offers supportive statements • Uses verbal and nonverbal signals to invite responses from others
Active listening	• Makes eye contact with the speaker • Uses an open posture • Stops other activities to listen • Paraphrases statements of others • Asks clarifying questions • Seeks and offers feedback
Conflict management	• Listens to the views of others • Avoids hurtful statements about others • States his or her own views without becoming defensive • Is able to identify personal concerns and the concerns of others • Accepts the group's decision graciously • Is able to resume the task

have a decreased ability to develop a theory of mind, a characteristic referred to as *mind blindness* (Baron-Cohen, Leslie, & Frith, 1985). For someone with autism, the assumption that "if I can't feel it, you can't feel it, and the way I perceive it is the way you perceive it" becomes an obstacle to relating to others or developing close social ties.

Researchers also postulate that the mirror neuron systems, discussed in Chapter 3, play a supporting role in developing a theory of mind (Sommerville & Decety, 2006). This suggests that empathy and the ability to take on different perspectives can emerge from exposure to the feelings of others and from experiences that foster differing points of view. It is clear that changes in brain activation are associated with a person's ability to perceive the thoughts and feelings of others, even when they are not experienced directly. Brain scans of children between the ages of 7 and 12 who were shown images of someone in pain or someone being intentionally hurt by someone else are consistent with the brain scans of adults shown the same images (Decety, Michalska, & Akitsuki, 2008).

Instructional Routines That Foster Interpersonal and Small-Group Skills

Students, then, are ready to learn interpersonal skills; teachers just need to provide them the opportunity. Learning to work well with others requires modeling, lots of practice, reflection, and refinement of skills. Making assumptions about what skills students already know or should have learned along the way is unfair and can result in a number of unexpected and negative consequences. In this section, we describe several routines for helping students gain competence in small-group interactions, from communicating clearly, to listening and responding to one another, to taking on different perspectives.

Thinking and Communicating with Clarity

Before sharing ideas with others, students must be able to organize and sharpen their own thoughts. Costa and Kallick (2000) identify this important skill, "thinking and communicating with clarity and precision," as one of the "habits of mind" necessary for students to tackle new problems successfully. Our experience suggests that this skill is particularly important to making group work productive, and it can be developed and validated in the process of learning cooperatively.

Graphic organizers are effective tools for helping students sort their thoughts before presenting them to others. A fair amount of research indicates that graphic organizers support student understanding, possibly because they provide learners with visual representations of the content at hand (Ives, 2007; Robinson, 1998). Also, these graphic tools generally require students to think critically about content as they sort through, evaluate, and identify the most essential information, and can help students clarify connections and relationships between concepts and ideas found in resources (Fisher & Frey, 2007).

Venn diagrams, webs, sequence maps, charts, and T-charts (see Figure 5.2) are all examples of basic graphic organizers that every student should know how to use. One key to getting the most out of these tools lies in students' choosing to use them rather than a teacher assigning them. In other words, teachers should not copy blackline masters of graphic organizers and require students to fill them out. Doing so would make completing them like doing a worksheet, which we know does not grow dendrites (Tate, 2003) or encourage branching thoughts. Instead, teachers should show students a variety of ways they might visually represent ideas and information and encourage students to select and use the one that best helps them to organize their thinking.

In Ms. Bruton's 7th grade history class, students regularly use graphic organizers in their group work. Ms. Bruton introduced a wide range of graphic tools and taught her students how to select specific ones appropriate for a task. During the class investigation of medieval life, Ms. Bruton provided each group with a range of texts in which they could find information about the assigned topic. Individual group members took notes as they read and presented their findings during their small-group discussion. Taylor created a web to organize his research about Charlemagne (see Figure 5.3).

During the roundtable discussion that was part of their productive group work, Taylor used his web to talk about what he had learned. As his peers asked questions and provided additional information, Taylor referred to his web and made plans to update it, as we can see from the following excerpt of their discussion:

Brooke: Did Charlemagne have any children?

Taylor: I don't know, but I can find out and tell you tomorrow.

Amanda: What does his name mean?

Taylor: He was really named Charles, but people called him Charlemagne, which means "Charles the Great," because he conquered so many places and people.

Figure 5.2	**Common Graphic Organizers**	
Type	**Description**	**Example**
Venn Diagram	Overlapping circles that illustrate similarities and differences between two concepts	
Web	A central word or phrase linked to supporting labels, concepts, and ideas	
Sequence/process map	A series of steps	
Chart/matrix	Rows and columns in table format that show relationships vertically and horizontally	
T-chart	A two-column table for grouping ideas into categories	

Figure 5.3 | **Student-Created Web**

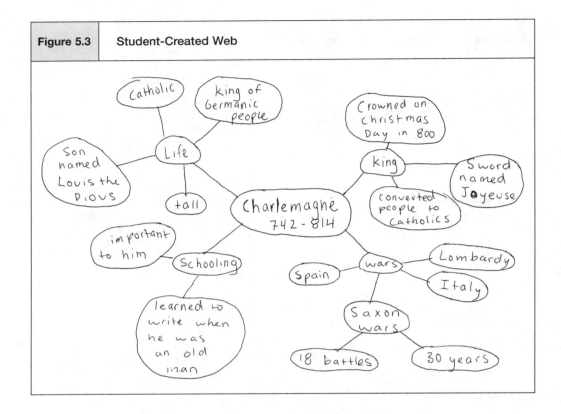

Active Listening

To interact as a group and build on each other's ideas, students must be able to listen to and understand their groupmates. Active listening is a system of techniques for focusing the listener, encouraging the speaker, and ensuring the listener understands what the speaker has said. Figure 5.4 lists these listening techniques and how to execute them.

Fourth grade teacher Mr. Tresman has given active listening a great deal of time and attention in his class and feels that these efforts are essential. He notes, "It's hard to work in a productive group if you don't really listen to what other people are saying."

Mr. Tresman also routinely assesses his own active listening skills: "It's difficult to plan [his group discussion comments] in advance, because it's not like you can write a script for yourself on being an active listener." Instead, he has drawn a chart that he leaves on the classroom's dry-erase board. It's titled "Was Mr. T. a good listener today? You decide!" and he gives himself a check mark in each of the following categories:

Figure 5.4	**Active Listening Techniques**		
What to Do	**Why Do It**	**How to Do It**	**Examples of What to Say**
Encourage	• To convey interest in what the speaker is discussing • To keep the person talking	• Nod, smile, and use other facial expressions. • Don't agree or disagree. • Use noncommittal words with positive tone of voice.	• "I see. . . ." • "Uh-huh. . . ." • "OK. . . ." • "Keep going. . . ."
Restate or clarify	• To show that you are listening and understand • To check your perception of the speaker's message	• Restate the basic ideas, emphasizing the facts. • Clarify points. • Don't "fake listen"!	• "If I understand correctly, your idea is . . ." • "I see what you mean." • "In other words, this is . . ." • "What did you mean when you said . . ."
Reflect or paraphrase	• To show the speaker that what he or she is saying is being heard • To show you understand the speaker's feelings	• Restate the other's basic feelings. • Respond to the other's main ideas.	• "So you feel that . . ." • "You must feel angry that . . ." • "I think you're very happy that . . ."
Summarize	• To pull important ideas, facts, and so on together • To establish a basis for further discussion • To review progress	• Restate, reflect, and summarize major ideas and feelings.	• "So would you say the key ideas are . . ." • "If I understand you, you're saying that . . ." • "Based on your presentation, would it be accurate to say that . . ."

- Asked a clarifying question
- Restated someone's idea
- Made eye contact with the speaker
- Asked a follow-up question
- Used friendly body language

At the end of the day, he tallies his score with the class and asks for a rating from 1 to 10 on his Good Listener scale. "The kids like the idea of grading me each day,"

Mr. Tresman remarks, "and it keeps me on my toes. Of course, we don't score every single interaction, because that would take too much time. Instead, I let them decide on a 15-minute time frame for collecting data. That way, I'm always changing the content area and the instructional arrangement."

When Mr. Tresman thought his students were ready to use active listening in their productive group work, he gave them the following checklist:

_____ Do you paraphrase what has been said before you respond?

_____ Do you ask for clarification when you do not understand something someone says?

_____ Do you encourage other people in the group to participate?

_____ Do you look at and make eye contact with others when they are talking to you?

_____ Do you give every member of the group an opportunity to speak?

_____ Do you watch body language and make sure others are not trying to speak or are frustrated?

The list both set the expectations for listening and provided scaffolding for good listening behaviors during group work.

Adrian, a student in Mr. Tresman's class, said of developing active listening skills, "I had to learn to listen and not just hear what others were saying." We know that this focus on active listening will serve Adrian well, both now, while he is in school, and later, in the workplace.

Responding to Peers

Asking a student to give constructive criticism to a peer can stretch even the most socially adept student. Student feedback often falls into one of two categories—either too polite to offer any substantial or useful suggestion or needlessly blunt and likely to hurt feelings. In their defense, most students have never been taught how to provide feedback to one another. As Jay Simmons (2003) reminds us, "Responders are taught, not born" (p. 684).

Peer feedback should be more of a response to a fellow student's work or idea than a judgment of it or of the student. For example, the kind of feedback that is most useful to a writer is reflecting back what was understood as a reader, asking questions to clarify the writer's purpose, and making suggestions that provide the writer with a sense of what he or she needs to do next (Simmons, 2003). Think of it less as "editing" and more as responding as a fellow reader, writer, or listener. The teacher's role is to model these kinds of responses and monitor their practice. Figure 5.5 breaks down steps for modeling peer response to writing, but the steps—praising, reflecting understanding, questioning, and suggesting—could be transferred to modeling peer responses to any type of student work.

A simple frame for younger students to use when giving constructive feedback is the "sandwich." In this model, students use three stages of conversation. The first layer consists of praise, with specific positive examples. Constructive criticism forms the "meat" of the discussion, with suggestions for improvement. Finally, the peer conference finishes with an identified next step.

After having the sandwich frame presented and modeled by 3rd grade teacher Marisol Ramirez, Nick's group practices giving feedback in a peer conference. Here is the group's response to Nick's reading of his report on turtles:

> *Clint:* I liked the details you gave. I especially liked how you told us that turtles can feel on their shell.
>
> *Nick:* Thanks. I didn't know that they could do that, but I found it in a book.
>
> *Brianna:* I agree that your details were good. The words were good, too. For example, I didn't know that the top and bottom of the shell had different names. I learned that *carapace* is the top shell and *plastron* is the bottom shell.
>
> *Nick:* Wow, thank you.
>
> *Brianna:* But I think you should redo your conclusion.
>
> *Nick:* Do you have specifics for me?
>
> *Brianna:* Well, I kinda thought that your introduction was more interesting than your conclusion. You only say what you already said. Maybe you could add some humor or ask a question at the end.

Figure 5.5	Peer Response Techniques	
Technique	**What the Teacher Does**	**What Students Do**
Sharing your writing	• Shares a piece of writing and asks for response • Shares rewrites tied to class response	• Offer comments on the teacher's writing
Clarifying evaluation vs. response	• Shows evaluation is of product • Response is to the writer	• Understand that response is personable and helpful
Modeling specific praise	• Shows how to tell what you like	• Understand that cheerleading as a reader is too general to be helpful
Modeling understanding	• Shows how to tell what you understood the piece to be about	• Understand that reflecting back the piece to the writer is helpful
Modeling questions	• Shows how to ask questions about what you didn't understand	• Understand that questions related to the writer's purpose are helpful
Modeling suggestions	• Shows how to suggest writing techniques	• Understand that a responder leaves a writer knowing what to do next
Whole-class response	• Moderates response by class to one classmate's piece	• Offer response • Hear the response of others • Hear what the writer finds helpful
Partner response	• Pairs up students in class to respond to pieces	• Practice response learned in whole-class session
Comment review	• Reads the comments of peers to writers • Suggests better techniques • Devises mini-lessons	• Get teacher feedback on comments
Response conference	• Speaks individually with students responding inappropriately	• Have techniques reinforced

Source: Simmons, J. (2003). Responders are taught, not born. *Journal of Adolescent and Adult Literacy, 46*(8), 684–693. Reprinted with permission of the International Reading Association (www.reading.org).

Clint: I agree. I don't want to sound mean or anything. It's really good, your paper. But you could make the reader really remember it if you did more work on the conclusion, like Brianna says. Could you read us the end again?

Nick: Yeah, OK. I sort of ran out of time at the end. Maybe I need some help on this part.

Nick's group gave useful feedback, pointing out specific things they liked and learned, and suggested a next step for him to take to improve the report. In turn, Nick accepted his peers' responses graciously.

Considering Different Perspectives

Another step in building students' interpersonal and social skills to facilitate productive group work is to have them practice considering situations and issues from different perspectives and then create opportunities for them to disagree with one another on a topic of substance. Collaborative learning is designed to expose students to multiple viewpoints, and it can build students' capacity to understand the perspective of others and craft a position for themselves.

For example, Sheridan Steelman at Northview High School in Michigan asked his 9th grade English students to use inquiry and research to analyze the decisions of Romeo and Juliet from different perspectives. Students studied *Romeo and Juliet* in class and read linking texts, such as Ovid's take on the myth of Pyramus and Thisbe. They also read and viewed information about adolescent brain development to further understand why the teenaged lovers in these stories might have made such poor choices. Students annotated their texts and then met in groups to discuss both the stories and the neuroscience. They addressed two questions, supplied by Mr. Steelman: "How has your brain matured over the last 10 years?" and "Do you make better decisions now than you did when you were younger?" Meeting in groups of four, the students supported their answers, listened to the perspectives of others, and then independently responded to this writing prompt: "How can potential consequences guide your decision making?"

Doug and Nancy also regularly get our high school students to try out different perspectives by creating a controversy. For 9th grade students in a unit on ethical and legal issues in health care, we adapt for group work a scenario from Lawrence

Kohlberg's classic measure of stages of moral development (Crain, 2005). In this story, a man breaks into a pharmacy to steal a life-saving medication for his sick wife because he doesn't have money to buy it. We ask our students to think carefully about this dilemma from the standpoint of the man, the sick woman, the pharmacy owner, the pharmaceutical company representative, and the police officer. The activity is set up as a jigsaw, with students belonging to a home group of five and each assuming a different role in the scenario. Students then meet in role-alike groups to craft their arguments.

The academic language skills required for secondary students include being able to engage in rhetorical modes of thinking and writing that promote thoughtful analysis of complex topics. The classic forms of rhetoric—*ethos* (the credibility of the author), *logos* (using facts and reasons to support claims), and *pathos* (appealing to the emotions)—frame most essays and date back to the time of Aristotle. These methods of argumentation underlie the formal academic writing necessary in fields ranging from the sciences to the arts, and they provide a very useful way for teachers to introduce students to differing points of view.

While many students can make arguments based on simple emotional appeals (pathos), they have less experience with using credibility (ethos) and reason (logos) to frame a position. This is why Doug and Nancy give them frequent opportunities to develop their own arguments and to listen to the perspectives of their peers. In their role-alike groups, students work on creating arguments using all three strategies and then meet in their home group to hear the positions of the other involved parties.

The notes on ethos, pathos, and logos arguments that students develop in their home groups provide the foundation for a class debate. Team members return to the role-alike groups to offer their rationale for why the man who broke into the pharmacy should be recommended for trial or why the charges should be dismissed. We assess the use of arguments and counterarguments throughout the debate. During the final class, each student writes an opinion paper and uses all three methods of argumentation to support his or her position.

Inside Three Classrooms

We began the chapter by discussing our innate, human desire to connect with one another and how our brains are designed and develop to support those connections. We have also examined several instructional routines for the modeling and practice of interpersonal skills. Now we will see how our three teachers use these skills to make group work more productive.

Ms. Allen, Elementary School Mathematics

Aida Allen's kindergarten students are proud of their growing knowledge of numbers and how to add them. Throughout the year, students have built their number sense and computational skills through several kinds of short, collaborative learning activities. These activities also have given the kindergartners a chance to develop their social skills. One of their favorite activities is called "Busy Bees." At the start of Busy Bees, Ms. Allen gives each child anywhere from one to five interlocking cubes to hold in one hand and a whiteboard and marker to hold in the other. Then, she gathers her students in the center of the classroom and reminds them of the rules for the activity:

> *Ms. Allen:* Remember you are all busy bumblebees, but you fly very slowly. That means that no one needs to bump into another bee.
>
> *Robert:* Bumping could hurt their feelings.
>
> *Ms. Allen:* That's right, Robert. Good remembering of other people's feelings. Remember that when you meet your partner, you say "hello" and say his or her name. When you're done, say "thank you" and use your partner's name again. People like to hear their names.

Ms. Allen goes on to explain today's task—partnering with another child to add up the total number of cubes between them. "You'll do this five times," she explains. "Each time you'll add up a different amount and write the equation on your whiteboard."

When Ms. Allen says, "Busy bees, fly!" the students shuffle their feet and make a buzzing sound in imitation of bumblebees. When she says, "Busy bees, land!" they stop moving and buzzing to greet their partners. They then lock their blocks together and write the equation on their boards. "Be helpful!" Ms. Allen reminds them. "Make sure your bee buddy has written down the answer correctly."

After repeating this process four more times, she tells the students to "Fly home!" and they return to their seats. Although these partnerships are brief, the focus on interpersonal skills creates a supportive and positive environment that makes the learning partnerships more productive.

Ms. Vogel, Middle School English

The students in Kathy Vogel's 7th grade English class were writing autobiographies and examining them as a means of self-discovery. Ms. Vogel began the unit by dragging a large footlocker into the classroom and inviting students to speculate about its contents.

Each day after that, she took one object out of the locker and told the personal story connected to it. Each object represented an important event in her life.

After telling the story, she wrote it down, modeling her writing process using a think-aloud approach (Davey, 1983). When the writing was complete, she asked students to provide peer responses to her autobiography so that she could improve it. "I didn't want them to edit," she remarked. "I wanted them to ask questions as a reader would, in order to help their fellow writer consider ideas." To this end, she led a class discussion to capture students' insights about what peer responses should look like and sound like. She constructed a T-chart and recorded their norms (e.g., write notes on a separate piece of paper, not on the story; share airtime).

Over the next several weeks, students paired up to consult with one another about drafts of their own autobiographies. They used a class-developed T-chart to shape their peer response discussions, and Ms. Vogel provided reinforcement by reviewing the chart at the beginning of each draft review meeting. Because Ms. Vogel spent time helping students identify and develop peer response skills, they got more out of their group work and produced better autobiographies.

Mr. Gibbs, High School History

Student-run seminars are a rich and regular part of Brian Gibbs's curriculum. They provide students with the opportunity to demonstrate what they know, clarify misunderstandings, and identify gaps in their knowledge. Plus, they are highly engaging and something students look forward to during each unit.

The seminars generally take two forms: character seminars and personal seminars. Character seminars, as we have seen in previous chapters, involve students' posing and responding to questions from the perspective of the historical character they have been assigned. Personal seminars follow the same format, only students discuss and debate ideas from their personal viewpoint. Before students can engage in productive discussions, however, they need to learn and practice group-discussion skills, such as active listening, disagreeing constructively, staying on topic, sharing the floor, backing up statements with evidence, and encouraging peers.

Mr. Gibbs teaches these skills one at a time. Early in the year, students brainstorm and list behaviors they think contribute to a productive discussion. Once the list is complete, Mr. Gibbs asks the students to discuss what the behavior "looks like" and what it "sounds like." For example, students usually include listening as an important part of a good discussion, but they have rarely been asked to think about what it looks like when someone is really listening. After asking students to describe what good listeners say (clarify statements, ask follow-up questions) and do (lean forward, make eye contact), Mr. Gibbs models those skills by simulating an interview, periodically stopping so that students can discuss the listening behaviors they observe.

Finally, students are given the chance to practice the skill with their peers. Depending on the skill or language levels of the students, the groups may be as small as two students engaging in a Think-Pair-Share or as large as a teacher-guided whole-group discussion. Throughout the structured practice, Mr. Gibbs stops the groups, asks them to gauge how well they are doing as listeners, and shares his own observations.

As the class begins to participate in character and personal seminars, Mr. Gibbs continues to assess and provide feedback on their discussion skills. To do this, he often uses a discussion-web graphic organizer. On the day of the seminar, all students gather in a single, large circle to review the questions they have prepared for the seminar discussion. While they do so, Mr. Gibbs makes a "map" of the discussion circle, drawing a circle on a piece of paper and, just outside it, jotting down students' names to show exactly where each is sitting. Once the discussion begins, Mr. Gibbs places his pen on the name of the first student to speak. When the next student speaks he draws a line from student 1 to student 2, then from student 2 to student 3, and so on. At the end of the discussion, the lines on the paper resemble a spider web.

After school, Mr. Gibbs makes a copy of the discussion web for every student and the next day asks students to look at the web and reflect on what it tells them about their participation. Did they monopolize the discussion (i.e., there are lots of lines to and from their name) or not participate at all (there are no lines to or from their name)? The discussion web is a valuable reflective tool for students and provides Mr. Gibbs with information about which students need help or encouragement setting participation goals. One student shared that she was scared at the beginning of the year. "I was used to just sitting in class and letting the teacher talk," she explains. "I didn't think anyone really wanted to hear what I had to say." She went on to describe how at first Mr. Gibbs encouraged her to share at least one thing during a discussion. "Now," she reports, "I feel totally comfortable sharing my ideas with the class."

6

Incorporating Group Processing

Legendary retired UCLA basketball coach John Wooden is nearly as famous for his ability to mentor young people as he is for his unmatched winning record. His former players speak affectionately about their coach's maxims for success, which apply both on and off the court. These include the gems "Failing to prepare is preparing to fail" and "Little things make big things happen." Above all, Coach Wooden understands that learning is continuous and that processing what has occurred is as important as the task itself. In his words, "It's what you learn after you know it all that counts." Yet this principle is often overlooked in classrooms during the rush to move on to the next unit of instruction. Wooden might caution, "Be quick, but don't hurry."

When it comes to building the skills of students who are engaged in productive group work, it is vital that they have an opportunity to process their experience after they've completed a task. They should take time to examine their contributions and those of their groupmates. Group work improves when students discuss and assess their interaction, the progress they made toward their goal, and what did and did not work, and then go on to talk about what they'll do differently in the future.

There are a number of ways groups can assess their progress and communicate their thoughts. Group processing can be as simple as writing down one thing the group did to encourage a student to participate, noting something a partner said that moved the work forward, rating how well the group used a targeted skill, or identifying one thing the group could do better next time.

The Neural Basis for Group Processing

Group processing is a critical component of collaborative learning not only for building group skills but also for developing *metacognition,* the ability to reflect on one's learning. An important element of metacognition is being able to plan an approach to a learning task and then executing that plan.

Teachers know that metacognitive skills evolve slowly and over many years, as does a student's *executive function.* You may have encountered this term in recent years, perhaps in relation to a student with a disability's difficulties with decision making, planning, and organization. Executive function represents a cluster of abilities typically required when circumstances change or when something unexpected occurs. Students who have difficulty with executive function may be able to perform familiar tasks well, but they struggle with new tasks or tasks that require them to use skills in a novel way. Think about how productive group work, with its attendant level of novelty and uncertainty, can tax the efforts of these learners.

Results of brain imaging studies indicate that many of the neural networks used to perform executive function tasks lie in the prefrontal cortex (the lobes behind the forehead) and develop over time as part of human growth. Neurons communicate by transmitting electrical impulses that trigger the release of molecules called neurotransmitters. As we discussed in Chapter 4, the speed at which neurons communicate increases greatly when they are wrapped in an insulating sheath called myelin. When nerves are repeatedly stimulated by activity, such as practicing the piano for hours, the myelin gets thicker. The thicker the myelin, the faster the signals travel. The growth of networks and myelination of the brain occurs in a roughly back-to-front manner, with prefrontal cortex maturation occurring in adolescence and young adulthood (Giedd et al., 1999). After peaking at about age 11 or 12, the number of neurons (gray matter) begins to decline. As children enter adolescence, there is both a rapid pruning of neurons involved in less frequently used networks and an increase in myelination of the well-traveled pathways (Choudhury, Charman, & Blakemore,

2008). All of this adding to and subtracting from may help explain why it is that adolescents can be the model of maturity one moment and seem totally devoid of common sense the next.

The neuroscience literature supports the behavioral research on the need for time and multiple opportunities to develop metacognitive and executive skills (Gilbert & Burgess, 2008). When you are shaking your head because you know you've taught a skill before, remember you are building up your students' myelin. Without the external support of instructional routines that foster metacognition and executive function, students would have a very difficult time developing these capacities.

Instructional Routines That Support Group Processing

Teachers can use several routines to help group members process experiences. Three we particularly recommend are self-monitoring questionnaires, learning logs, and roundtable activities.

Self-Monitoring Questionnaires

To engage in purposeful group processing, students must first be able to reflect on their own learning. *Self-monitoring,* sometimes called self-regulation, involves setting goals and evaluating one's progress, recognizing problem-solving skills, and reporting behaviors that help or hinder one's learning. Self-monitoring is also linked to the transfer of skills from one setting to another (Billing, 2007), which is part of executive function.

While these monitoring behaviors may sound complex, they can be simplified to meet the developmental stage of the student. For example, elementary students might circle a series of smiling and frowning faces in response to questions about their learning, while older students might use a Likert scale, rating their agreement to statements about their work from 1 to 5, to evaluate their progress (see Figure 6.1 for an example of both types of questionnaires).

Teachers of high school students often include open-ended responses or scenarios on a questionnaire. We like these questions developed by Lan (2005) for his study on self-monitoring in students in grades 4–12:

- You finish a day of school and go home. You are reviewing and previewing for classes. There is always something else you want to do, so you

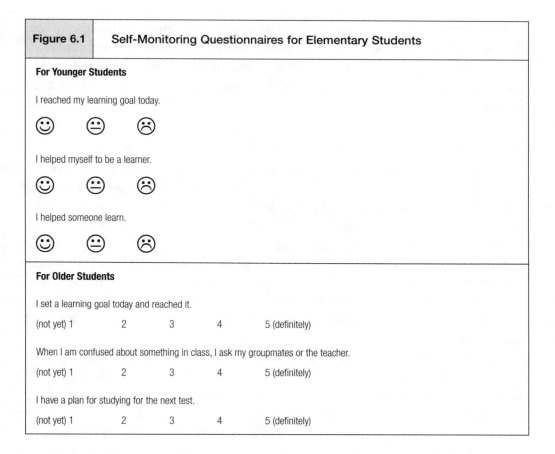

| Figure 6.1 | Self-Monitoring Questionnaires for Elementary Students |

For Younger Students

I reached my learning goal today.

☺   😐   ☹

I helped myself to be a learner.

☺   😐   ☹

I helped someone learn.

☺   😐   ☹

For Older Students

I set a learning goal today and reached it.

(not yet) 1   2   3   4   5 (definitely)

When I am confused about something in class, I ask my groupmates or the teacher.

(not yet) 1   2   3   4   5 (definitely)

I have a plan for studying for the next test.

(not yet) 1   2   3   4   5 (definitely)

quit studying when you think you have studied enough. How do you know you are ready for the classes?

- You will have a quiz in a course tomorrow, and you are preparing for the quiz. There is always something else you want to do, so you quit studying when you think you have studied enough. How do you know you are ready for the quiz?

- You will have a final examination in a course, and you have been studying for the exam for days. There is always something else you want to do, so you quit studying when you think you have studied enough. How do you know you are ready for the final exam? (p. 113)

Such open-ended questions incorporate several elements of learning, including study habits, effort, and use of texts and people as resources. Combined with closed-response questions, they can illuminate important habits of mind for the teacher and student. These self-reflection questionnaires establish a common basis for discussion during group processing.

Learning Logs

Learning logs are designed to encourage students to chronicle their learning across several days or weeks. Much like a diary, a learning log is meant to capture moments in time as students reflect upon what they understand, find confusing, or have questions about. As researcher Jeannie K. Wright (2005) notes, "[My learning log is] a discussion with myself on paper" (p. 507).

Learning logs are used during the clinical phase of many professions, including teaching, law, and medicine. In particular, they are valued as a way to promote reflective thinking as the learner acquires new skills and dispositions. However, this value is only realized when learning logs are used as a reflective tool and not as a catalog of experiences.

The parameters for what to record in a learning log can vary depending on the age of the student and the teaching purpose and discipline involved. Younger students are more likely to use pictures to show learning, such as illustrating their growing knowledge of a map of their neighborhood. Reading and language arts teachers often favor a split note-taking approach in logs, with students writing notes on their learning on the right side of the page and, after reviewing the notes, writing questions to themselves on the left side. Science students often illustrate their logs, for example, making detailed comparative representations of animal and plant cell structures. More traditionally, learning logs are text based, with each entry dated. In many cases, the teacher offers a question for students to reflect upon and compose a response to in their log. For example:

• What was the most interesting thing you learned today? How did you learn? Did you learn by reading, doing, or discussing?

• Describe three ways you helped yourself remember today's information.

• How did you lend a hand to someone else today?

• What still seems confusing? What will you do next to clear up your confusion?

- How does this topic relate to something you've already learned in this class? In another class?

- What is your study plan?

Remember that the value of learning logs is diminished without a plan for learners to review them across a series of entries. Group-processing discussions provide the perfect opportunity for this kind of review. The logs can be used in group-processing discussions simply by asking students to use them in supporting their statements about their own and the group's learning. For example, a group-processing question about the different ways students helped other members of the group can include evidence found in the learning logs. By asking students to revisit their log entries, the teacher creates the conditions needed for reflective thinking. Students may see patterns in their behaviors emerging over time or discover how much they've grown or improved in a specific area. A teacher can even ask students to color-code their responses with highlighter pens. For example, they might use green to mark evidence of learning, yellow to mark questions or points of confusion, and pink to indicate times when they got in the way of their own learning. These pattern exercises with learning logs can lead to richer and more reflective conversations among groups of learners.

Roundtable Activities

In their 2001 book *Making Task Groups Work in Your World,* Hulse-Killacky, Killacky, and Donigian note that while time for reflection and debriefing is essential to group work, group processing is often skipped because the focus on the task itself is seen as paramount. They also describe many groups' aversion to reflection as "dread . . . of touchy-feely time" (p. 106). Interestingly, their book is written for a business audience, although it accurately describes the dynamics present in many classrooms, especially secondary ones. They recommend using a *roundtable activity* to allow each member to reflect on the group's work, and they suggest these topics for discussion:

- Name something that surprised or confused you.

- Identify something you learned that you will use in another class.

- Describe one thing you will do to prepare for the next task.

- Name one approach that worked for you and one that did not.

- Discuss something to be celebrated.

Because 12th grade statistics teacher Mr. Halloran has his students working in study groups for the entire year, he requires that they roundtable after each unit of study. "I'm getting them ready for their college classes," he explains. "I know that next year they'll end up relying on the cohesiveness of their study groups." On the day before each major test, each study group spends about 15 minutes discussing focus questions related to the ways they worked together. "I want them to notice their own learning and think about their contributions to the group," says Halloran. When they take the test the following day, students find two questions related to their study habits and group work. The first asks them to report the amount of time they spent studying alone and with the group outside of class. (According to Mr. Halloran, their responses are frightfully honest.) The second question asks them to estimate the grade they will receive on the test. "It's a good way for me to see how closely their own estimations are aligning with their performance," Mr. Halloran notes. "I want them to understand that math ability isn't something you're born with, it is a function of the amount of time and effort you put into it."

Inside Three Classrooms

Knowing that reflection is an important part of making group work productive, our three example teachers have incorporated group processing in their students' group work. They allow time for students to assess their effort and provide support and guidance for student self-evaluation by asking prompting questions, using assessment rubrics and learning logs, and establishing specific times for reflecting and conferencing throughout a long task. Their efforts give their students the opportunity to learn about themselves as learners and to set goals for improvement.

Ms. Allen, Elementary School Language Arts

During her students' 5th grade year, Aida Allen introduced literature circles to promote meaningful discussion of longer texts. She was interested in fostering choice in her classroom and found that this instructional routine worked well for meeting the interests of her students. Every three to four weeks, she profiled books on a common theme that she'd selected across a range of reading levels and gave a brief book talk for each. For example, for a social studies unit on westward expansion, she chose *Riding Freedom* by Pam Muñoz Ryan; *Across the Wide and Lonesome Prairie: The Oregon Trail Diary of Hattie Campbell* by Kristiana Gregory; *Caddie Woodlawn* by Carol Ryrie Brink; *Prairie Visions: The Life and Times of Solomon Butcher* by Pam Conrad; and Scott O'Dell's *Sing Down the Moon*. This selection of books offered different perspectives related to gender, region, and position and included both fiction and nonfiction. After hearing about each book, students ranked them in order of their preference, with Ms. Allen having a final say about the composition of each group. She does this to ensure that each member of a literature circle group is reading a book at a suitable level of difficulty (and in doing so, differentiates the task by both interest and readiness). If a student wanted to read a book that was not challenging enough, for example, she'd steer the student to his or her more appropriate second or third choice.

Because the book groups change with every new title, her students must work with a variety of classmates throughout the year. The changing composition of groups challenges the students' ability to reflect on their own learning and discuss it with others. In an effort to promote reflective conversation about their group participation, Ms. Allen has expanded the role of the "discussion director" of each group to include facilitating group processing. Each Friday, Ms. Allen gives the day's discussion directors a list of questions to introduce in the group. On one Friday during the westward expansion unit, groups received these questions:

1. What was our best discussion this week? Why?
2. What was the hardest discussion we had? Why?
3. How will we use what we learned about our best discussion and our hardest discussion to improve next week?

The students reading *Riding Freedom* quickly agreed that the best discussion they had was on Wednesday, when they met to talk about the chapter in which Charlotte, the protagonist, is revealed to the other characters as a girl and not the boy that she had pretended to be. "I couldn't wait to talk to you," said Christopher to the other members of his group, "because I wanted to hear what you thought about it." After a few minutes spent remembering Wednesday's great discussion, Beto, the group's discussion director, asked the second question, about the hardest discussion. After a long silence, Adriana said, "I guess that would be Monday." She then admitted that she had forgotten to read the chapter over the weekend so she couldn't really participate in that day's discussion. Two other students immediately confessed to the same thing, and after looking at one another, they giggled in embarrassment. "It wasn't fair that we let each other down," Beto commented. "You can't talk about a book you didn't read."

Discussion of the third question started quickly, as the students realized that the best thing to do next was to remember to do the reading this weekend. "I can call anyone, if they want me to," volunteered Adriana. "I promise I won't forget!"

Ms. Vogel, Middle School Humanities

Although the students had presented their *Larry King Live* interviews, the work on this project was not finished for students in Kathy Vogel's 7th grade humanities class. Ms. Vogel had used the presentation rubric students created at the beginning of the project (see Figure 6.2) to evaluate their interview performances. Now she asked each partner group to do the same. Ms. Vogel videotaped the interviews so partners could watch their performance and use the rubric to discuss their work together. The rubric gave the partners common language and a starting point for their conversation. Once the pump had been primed, the group was ready to tackle

Figure 6.2	Presentation Rubric		
Factor	**Expert Performance**	**Proficient Performance**	**Novice Performance**
Voice	Strong, clear voice	Acceptable volume and clarity	Weak, unclear voice
Vocabulary	Consistent with the character interviewed	Some is consistent with the character interviewed	Not consistent with the character being interviewed
Nonverbal communication	Gestures and facial expression is consistently strong and adds to the interview	Attempt at gestures and facial expression is evident and contributes somewhat to the interview	Nonverbal communication is lacking and does not contribute to the interview
Acting	Stays in character and uses props effectively; very natural and credible	Mostly stays in character; fairly natural and credible	Does not stay in character; not a credible performance

Source: Courtesy of Kathy Vogel.

the more valuable part of the discussion: reflecting on what worked, what didn't work, and what they might do differently next time.

Ms. Vogel also asked the partners to use their learning log notes to support their comments about the ways they worked together. Students had kept logs over the course of their partner work on the interviews, and these logs contained their responses to reflection questions posted throughout the project. At various times, Ms. Vogel asked them to consider what they were doing to help themselves and to check with their partner to find out what might be confusing to him or her. During group processing, these notes helped to clear up the cloudy memories of partners who were not able to accurately recall the status of their work at a given point. The combination of videos, rubrics, and learning logs helped partners focus their reflective discussions on evidence of their learning and promoted metacognitive awareness. The feedback encouraged students to continually improve as they made plans for future work.

Mr. Gibbs, High School History

For Brian Gibbs, teaching students the importance and value of examining individual and group behaviors begins with the first group activity of the school year. As students work together, Mr. Gibbs moves throughout the groups, noting interactions, comments, and group behaviors. Following a whole-class discussion, students are asked to respond in writing to four questions:

1. What contributions did I make?
2. What additional contributions could I have made?
3. What worked well in our group?
4. What is one thing that could have been improved?

Mr. Gibbs then shares some of his observations. This first exposure to self- and group reflection is low-key, but it establishes a pattern that will be repeated throughout the course.

As the year progresses, Mr. Gibbs changes the types of individual and group assessments he uses. Modifying the criteria chart for evaluating a final project to make it a self-monitoring tool has been a successful technique, enabling students to measure their group's progress as they work. For example, as part of a unit on the Mexican Revolution, each group was assigned a different historical character.

Groups were expected to thoroughly research their character and develop a genuine understanding of that character beyond the usual historical facts. Students explored what motivated their character and made him or her a hero and demonstrated their knowledge of the character by creating a life-sized model that they presented to the entire class. For example, to demonstrate their insights into what might have motivated Emiliano Zapata to fight for land reform for Mexican peasants, one group attached a paper heart to their life-size model. On the reverse side of that heart, they had listed facts about Zapata's early childhood that they believed drove him to become the leader he was: the intense poverty he witnessed growing up, conflicts he observed between villagers and landowners, and his reported fluency in the indigenous Nahuatl language.

Mr. Gibbs turned the chart he would use to evaluate the groups' final product and presentation into a group-processing tool. He included in the criteria chart questions to help groups assess how they were working together, and he called it "a group progress report" (see Figure 6.3).

Figure 6.3	Group Progress Report and Criteria Chart

Group Name: _____   **Your Name:** _____

A. The Most Important Facts   **Progress Check-in Date:** _____

The 10 most important facts chosen from the life of your character are accurate, compelling, and describe the importance of your character in history. They are described in at least 10 complete sentences.

Major Weakness	Moderate Weakness	Strength and Weakness	Moderate Strength	Major Strength
1	2	3	4	5

Specific things our team is doing that are working well for this part of our project include:

Specific suggestions I have that will improve this part of our project include:

Figure 6.3	Group Progress Report and Criteria Chart (*continued*)

B. The Body Parts   **Progress Check-in Date:** _____

The five body parts chosen give deep insight and understanding into why your revolutionary character made the choices she/he did and help us understand what she/he saw, what was in her/his heart, what she/he was thinking about, and so on. The body parts illustrate your understanding through symbols and through your written words. Each body part has an explanation of at least eight well-written, well-thought-out sentences.

Major Weakness	Moderate Weakness	Strength and Weakness	Moderate Strength	Major Strength
1	2	3	4	5

Specific things our team is doing that are working well for this part of our project include:

Specific suggestions I have that will improve this part of our project include:

C. Why Is Your Character a Hero?   **Progress Check-in Date:** _____

Arguments and information are used well to explain how your character can be seen as a hero.

Major Weakness	Moderate Weakness	Strength and Weakness	Moderate Strength	Major Strength
1	2	3	4	5

Specific things our team is doing that are working well for this part of our project include:

Specific suggestions I have that will improve this part of our project include:

(continued)

Figure 6.3	Group Progress Report and Criteria Chart (*continued*)

D. The Character   **Progress Check-in Date:** _____

The Mexican Revolutionary Character that you created is lifelike in every respect and artistically well created.

Major Weakness	Moderate Weakness	Strength and Weakness	Moderate Strength	Major Strength
1	2	3	4	5

Specific things our team is doing that are working well for this part of our project include:

Specific suggestions I have that will improve this part of our project include:

E. Articulation and Explanation   **Progress Check-in Date:** _____

Students speak well and clearly. Each team member speaks an equal amount of time. Students are able to answer all questions posed to them.

Major Weakness	Moderate Weakness	Strength and Weakness	Moderate Strength	Major Strength
1	2	3	4	5

Specific things our team is doing that are working well for this part of our project include:

Specific suggestions I have that will improve this part of our project include:

Source: Courtesy of Brian Gibbs.

Groups regularly evaluated their work using the chart and checked in with Mr. Gibbs to assess the quality of their work and how well they were working together and to discuss how to change course before it was too late. By engaging in group processing during the project—looking at what was working and what needed to be improved at each step of the way—students were able to examine how changes in the group's interaction affected their productivity and the quality of their work.

7

Getting Started:
Questions and Answers

We have talked in depth about planning, guiding, and assessing productive group work. Now we want to answer what we know are the questions teachers most frequently ask about groups. These questions center around three concerns: group formation, providing content for groups, and introducing group work to the classroom. We hope the answers will provide you with some practical tools for getting started.

Group Formation

Should Students Be Grouped by Ability?

The short answer is no—students should not be grouped by ability for productive group work. In fact, ability-based (or homogeneous) groups run counter to the evidence on the effectiveness of productive group work. As we noted in the Introduction, groups are, on average, smarter than any single member. As part of their interaction, group members share information and experiences, thus building each others' background knowledge.

Research on ability-based "tracking" shows that this practice does not lead to increased achievement and can be harmful in terms of students' self-esteem and self-efficacy (Oakes, 2005). It is also important to recognize that most people are not ability grouped outside of school. In the world of work, groups interact and have to be productive in a number of ways and in a variety of situations. In most organizations, you don't get to pick the other members of your department or project teams, and being able to collaborate with others of varying skill levels, interests, and talents is essential to success.

That's not to say that there is no place for ability grouping within a classroom where students have different readiness levels. When the teacher is there to guide instruction, and we mean *physically* present with the learners in the group, it makes sense to have students with common learning needs working together so that the teacher can provide additional instruction, guided practice, or other kinds of targeted support. Homogeneous groups are also appropriate when the teacher has differentiated a task to accommodate students' instructional needs—that is, has designed different group activities to help students of varying readiness levels master the same content. For example, a teacher might design a literature circle in which homogeneous groups use different sets of materials, choosing from a range of texts selected to suit the independent reading levels of each group's members.

What Is the Best Way to Form Mixed-Ability Groups?

Most teachers are aware of the large body of research on the difficulties that arise from homogeneous grouping, especially as it relates to the suppression of achievement levels for struggling learners (e.g., Meijnen & Guldemond, 2002; Oakes, 2005). However, a poorly structured heterogeneous group can also be damaging. In particular, as Bennett and Cass (1988) found, when groups have a higher number of high-achieving students compared to the number of lower-achieving students, the tendency is for the majority to take control of the task and complete it with little regard to the learning of the members who need more time and repetition. In fact, these researchers found that when groups were structured at a ratio of one high-achieving student for every two lower-achieving ones, more talk resulted.

Mixed groups are most commonly formed in three ways: by *student choice,* by *random choice,* and by *teacher choice.* Allowing students to form their own groups—based on common interests, for example—can be a way to increase student engagement in a task. And groups based on student choice often work well for projects that must be completed outside of school simply as a matter of practicality. It's often easier for students who live near one another, or are already friends, to get together after school or on weekends to complete project work. However, student choice can be problematic for productive group work. Ideally, there should be a variety of student interests and skills in each group, which may or may not happen when students choose who they'll work with or what they'll work on.

Randomly chosen groups work well when interacting with a range of peers is helpful for the goal, such as when the group task relates to exploring attitudes and opinions. Having said that, randomly formed groups have the same drawbacks as student-formed ones—namely, that the groups may not have a sufficient range of experience and interests to complete the task.

This is why we generally recommend teacher-choice groups and often use an alternate ranking system to formulate them. This entails reviewing collected assessment data and composing a list of students in rank order of their academic scores and social skills, yielding a cumulative overall score. For example, we might rank a student as number 1 in academic skills but number 21 in social skills, for an overall score of 22.

Here's how it works. To form the groups, refer to the overall scores, rank order students from highest to lowest, and divide the list in two equal portions. For instance, students 1–15 would be on the first list, and students 16–30, on the second. When forming groups of two, partner student 1 with student 16, student 2 with student 17, and so on. When forming groups of four, you would invite students 1, 2, 16, and 17 to work together; students 3, 4, 18, and 19 to work together; and so on. This approach gives you partners who are heterogeneous yet not so far apart that they are likely to have difficulty bridging the divide. Of course, always review groups formed through ranking systems with a practical eye for factors like student compatibility. If two students have had a conflict or past difficulty working together, it might not be a good idea to put them in the same group. While not completely foolproof, this approach does give you a starting point for systematic group formation.

How Many Students Should Be in a Group?

Our rule of thumb is four. Of course, we recognize that classrooms don't always divide equally into groups of four. There might be a group or two of five students or a group or two of three students. We don't group two students together unless we're specifically engaged in partner or dyad work.

Our experience mirrors research findings that the larger groups get, the more students are excluded from the conversation. Fay, Garrod, and Carletta (2000) note that when group size was 10, "communication is like monologue and members are influenced most by the dominant speaker" (p. 481). As teachers, that's clearly not what we want. We need to keep group size small enough to ensure that every student benefits from participating.

The length of time needed for the task is also an important factor to consider. Generally speaking, shorter tasks require smaller groups, because otherwise there won't be adequate time to get input from everyone. Hence, short discussions work best for groups of just two because three or four people will not get adequate "airtime" in a two-minute limit. Long projects (especially those that continue for a week or more) can sustain groups of five or six students because there will be more opportunities for them to interact.

Groups of four are great because they provide differing viewpoints, a wider breadth of skills, and enough social cushioning to allow for high-quality projects. But the ultimate determination of group size should be the nature of the task or project. A Think-Pair-Share requires just two students, while a project on the history of the tango may need a group of five: two pairs of dancers and the moderator telling the story.

How Long Should Groups Stay Together?

This is a complex question. The answer depends, to a significant degree, on the types of tasks students complete as part of their productive group work. Some tasks are one-time events, and students should be regrouped following the completion of the task. Other tasks, such as reciprocal teaching and book clubs, require students to develop communication patterns, and thus the groups should be together longer. We tend to keep groups together for about six weeks to complete most of the kinds of projects outlined in this book.

Of course, every teacher should feel free to move individual students from group to group. Sometimes, groups should be reformed for behavioral reasons, and sometimes groups just don't gel. Remember, too, our recommendation that groups be formed based on formative assessment information. This means that you'll want to regularly collect formative assessment data—via tests, observation, questioning, student writing, and other projects or performances—to gain insight into students' levels of understanding and factor this into your grouping decisions and group adjustments.

What Should I Do When a Group Doesn't Function Well?

The first thing to determine when you see a group isn't working out is whether the difficulty is related to a particular episode, such as a disagreement among group members about how to approach the task. In such situations, helping the group clear its particular hurdle—here, reach a decision—is the best approach.

In other cases, it may be the task itself—unclear, too difficult, not challenging enough—that is causing the problem. In these cases, fall back on your instructional design. If the group is not ready to take on the task, you'll need to do some more guided instruction with them. If this proves insufficient, assume more of the cognitive responsibility and model, model, model.

And in some situations, a personality mismatch among students in the group may be the source of the group's struggle. Here, consider reconstituting the groups, and provide additional support to any student who is having trouble with the interpersonal skills required. That student might need some additional scaffolds, such as task cards or a checklist of items to address. Above all, resist the urge to allow a student to work alone. Although it may be the easy way out, it deprives that student of the opportunity to learn the necessary habits needed in a productive work group. After all, these students may be the ones who need the most modeling and practice working with others. Remember, school is a student's primary opportunity for learning group skills. If a student doesn't learn and practice them in class, he or she may never develop them.

Providing Content for Groups

Should All Groups Be Learning the Same Content?

If by *content* we mean the theme, objectives, or standards being addressed, the answer is yes, all groups should be learning the same content. We agree with Carol Ann Tomlinson, who notes, "There is benefit to holding what students learn relatively steady, while changing how we give access to the content to match student needs" (2001, p. 72). For example, if a class is focused on tectonic plates, all of the students in the room need to understand the ways in which the plates move and the impact that this movement has on our planet, such as volcanic eruptions and earthquakes. This is essential knowledge that all students in the class must acquire. Although the instructional approach a teacher takes to ensure all students meet this standard may vary according to student needs, the standard itself must be the same for all. Holding the standards constant is especially important for students who have traditionally been given an alternative curriculum within a general education classroom, such as students with learning disabilities and English language learners.

Although all student groups in a classroom should be focused on the same learning outcomes, instructional adjustments may be necessary to help all students master that curriculum. We definitely advocate differentiating resources and other materials to suit varying student needs, interests, and skill levels. For example, in a 10th grade world history class, the teacher asked her student groups to explore the question "How did World War II and the Holocaust affect people who did not fight?" She knew that she would boost the quality of the discussion by providing students with a variety of resource materials, including the textbook, a videotaped interview with a Holocaust survivor, and a selection of letters and diary entries written during the time. By providing source materials that varied in format and complexity, she was able to ensure all students could access the content without compromising the content's integrity.

How Do I Accommodate the Mixed Skills and Abilities Inherent in Heterogeneous Groups?

It's up to you, the teacher, to provide groups a variety of ways to access content so that students, no matter their skill level, can participate in the group's learning. Differentiation is the answer, and there are a number of excellent resources available on the topic, including Tomlinson's *The Differentiated Classroom* (1999), *How to Differentiate Instruction in Mixed-Ability Classrooms* (2001), and *Fulfilling the Promise of the Differentiated Classroom* (2003). Here are just a few ideas to get you started.

Text selection is one of the most important variables teachers can manipulate to facilitate students' understanding, and we think it is the best place to begin differentiating group work. Most of us have heard the educational axiom "You can't learn much from books you can't read" (Allington, 2002, p. 16). Yet students across the country are regularly assigned books that are far above their reading level. And it's done with the best intentions. Some teachers mistakenly believe that requiring an 8th grader who reads at the 4th grade level to read the 8th grade textbook will help him catch up faster. Others worry that poor readers will fall further behind if they don't read the same book everyone else is reading. And still other teachers have limited access to reading materials and therefore have to make do with what is available. The problem with all of these scenarios is that they impede student learning.

The range of student reading levels in a given classroom or group requires teachers to plan their lessons in a different fashion. Wise practitioners plan for a span of four grade levels (two below grade level, one at grade level, and one above grade level) in order to increase access to the content. Textbooks are written at an assigned grade level, which is problematic for students who read below that level. For these students, textbook reading assignments are often a frustrating series of missed learning opportunities. Not only do they miss out on the information contained in the book, but they are also unable to fully engage in any of the reading-based group tasks or follow-on activities. The gold standard for reading is the ability to comprehend, that is, to make meaning of the words on the page. But when text is at a frustration level for some students (typically defined as reading 89 percent or less of the words correctly), comprehension is compromised. Students suffer a "double whammy" when they are asked to read at the frustration level—they both fail to improve their reading skills and slip further behind their classmates in content knowledge.

In planning productive group tasks, teachers have to consider the instructional materials and texts they use. Having students meet in groups to struggle through hard books is not the answer. Instead, it's a matter of first determining the range and types of text that students need to develop their conceptual understanding and then incorporating these texts into the productive group work tasks that we assign. Remember, the textbook is merely one source; it does not define the curriculum itself. Consider the perspective offered by a textbook: It serves as a summary of the *textbook authors'* knowledge of the content. While valuable, it is several degrees removed from the primary source information used by the authors in developing the textbook.

We encourage teachers to consider all the many alternatives for conveying content information. Try including some biographies in your group work, or diaries, letters, and autobiographies, which give students a taste of primary sources. Search out Web sites that have creditable host institutions, include accurate and up-to-date information, offer material spanning a variety of reading levels, and are easy to use. Then create a computer learning station for group rotations, with those Web sites bookmarked for exploration. And don't forget to consider the rich array of nontextual resources, including audio and video, guest speakers, and trips to places of interest, which give students a chance to explore a topic in a real-life context.

We have also found that the arts make an excellent entry point to content for many students. Children's literature and young adult fiction cover a range of topics and historical periods from different points of view and at different reading levels. Poetry that is related to science, math, or social studies can also be very effective. There are collections of poems about weather, seasons, insects, multiplication, and even algebra! And don't forget picture books. They provide all learners, including older students, with a different perspective on topics across content areas and have been used successfully in middle school classrooms to encourage reluctant readers to participate in content area instruction (Cassady, 1998; Fisher & Frey, 2008b). Music has also been found to be a powerful way to motivate students to read (Towell, 1999/2000). We've seen students pore over song lyrics and search out books related to the songs they like. Alvermann and Hagood (2000) found that introducing analysis of popular music into instruction not only increases students' interest but can increase critical-thinking skills such as analysis, synthesis, and evaluation.

Introducing Group Work

How Do I Prepare Students for Group Work?

Our experience suggests that teachers start small, with lots of short, partner-driven conversations, so that they can foster the interpersonal skills needed for more complex tasks. In the same way that jumping on the gas pedal consumes too much fuel, beginning group work with a very complex task will tend to tax both you and your learners.

Begin from the first day with multiple opportunities to interact successfully. Give students the language of sharing ideas by constructing frames that support their academic conversations. For younger children, practice may focus on turn taking and listening to one another. We will sometimes give partners a "talking chip" that they pass back and forth as they converse. We encourage older students to use more formal academic language as a means for engaging in deeper conversations. In addition, we find this practice to be an important precursor to academic writing, rhetoric, and argumentation. Here are some recommended language frames for productive group work discussions:

Explaining Ideas

- The main idea is _____.

- The reason I know this is because _____.

- This is like _____ and different from _____.

Checking for Understanding

- Does that make sense to you?

- Is there a part that is confusing?

- Can you repeat it in your own words?

Asking for Clarification

- Can you explain that again?

- Could you show me where you found that information?

- I understood _____, but I didn't understand _____. Can you help me?

Helping a Person Get "Unstuck"

- Show the person where you found information.

- Ask the person to explain what he or she knows.

- Use another resource (book, computer, teacher).

- Ask someone else for help in explaining the information.

Disagreeing Politely

- I know that you think _____ while I think _____. I'll explain why I believe _____ and then you tell me why you believe _____.

- I agree with you because _____. I disagree with you about _____. Could both of us be right?

- That's an interesting idea. I disagree with you about _____. Can you tell me why you think _____?

Using Each Other's Ideas

- (Student's name) _____ said _____ and it reminded me of _____.

- Our ideas are similar because _____.

- Our ideas are different because _____.

- We could use _____ and _____ to explain _____.

- Here's a new idea that uses _____'s thoughts and _____'s thoughts.

Remember that teacher modeling is essential to meaningful learning conversations. As you lead class discussions, pause from time to time to spotlight your use of these techniques. For instance, before asking a clarifying question of a student, tell the class, "I am not sure I understand completely. When I don't understand, I ask another question." As well, think aloud to explain how you use specific language frames. Formulate questions using these structures, and then let the entire class participate in the answer. Finally, turn the tables and allow the students to construct specific questions to pose to you. These questions from students needn't go on for long, but the regular use of modeling to frame discussion techniques will build students' capacity to sustain longer conversations during group work.

How Do I Introduce Group Work into My Classroom?

Teachers typically use productive group work in one of two ways: students work on the same task in small groups, or they rotate through a variety of tasks in small groups.

The latter method, variously referred to as *centers, workshops, learning stations,* or *experiences,* is a common feature of elementary classrooms and secondary English classrooms. A goal of this model is to create time for the teacher to provide guided instruction to one small group of students at a time while the other groups are engaged in collaborative work. Students working productively in this model are usually moving through a host of experiences that are repeated each week. The teacher has a format pattern in mind (e.g., independent reading, literature circles, research, or writing) and coordinates the format, as appropriate, to the lesson content.

When introducing various kinds of group work to students—the procedures of a literature circle, say, or of a research center—the teacher must be certain to model how each works before the whole class and then provide guided practice through the strategic use of cues, prompts, and questions. Students then work in groups, while the teacher circulates through the groups in order to address any problems. This might include re-teaching the steps of the group process, reteaching content, or both. Introduce subsequent stations one at a time, while continuing to implement previously taught stations. In our own work, over the course of 20 days of instruction at the beginning of the school year, we model and practice up to five stations in an orderly fashion, allowing time for students to build capacity and stamina. A typical implementation schedule looks something like this:

Day 1. Collaborative learning lesson: *What are the goals and expectations of group learning?*

Day 2. Introduce Station 1. Provide focus lesson and guided practice.

Day 3. Practice, circulate, and evaluate Station 1. Observe students and evaluate procedures.

Day 4. Introduce Station 2. Provide focus lesson and guided practice.

Day 5. Practice, circulate, and evaluate Station 2. Observe students and evaluate procedures.

Day 6. Implement Stations 1 and 2. Divide class in half, then switch.

Day 7. Collaborative learning lesson: *How do you get help when your group is stuck?*

Day 8. Introduce Station 3. Provide focus lesson and guided practice.

Day 9. Practice, circulate, and evaluate Station 3. Observe students and evaluate procedures.

Day 10. Implement Stations 1–3. Introduce schedule and complete three rotations.

Day 11. Assessment day. Implement Stations 1–3. Assess individuals or small groups.

Day 12. Collaborative learning lesson: *How do you offer, accept, decline, and ask for help?*

Day 13. Introduce Station 4. Provide focus lesson and guided practice.

Day 14. Practice, circulate, and evaluate Station 4. Observe students and evaluate procedures.

Day 15. Implement Stations 1–4. Introduce schedule and complete three rotations.

Day 16. Assessment day. Implement Stations 1–4 and assess individuals or small groups.

Day 17. Introduce Station 5. Provide focus lesson and guided practice.

Day 18. Practice, circulate, and evaluate Station 5. Observe students and evaluate procedures.

Day 19. Collaborative learning lesson: *How do you know you are finished? What do you do next?*

Day 20. Introduce teacher-directed station with the five collaborative stations.

What of the other format for productive group work, having all groups working on the same task at the same time? While the introduction for this format is shorter in duration, the overall structure is similar. Beginning with easier and shorter tasks, model how the work is to be completed and provide a bit of guided practice so you can check for understanding. As students shift into group-work mode, use the time to provide on-the-spot guided instruction. If you notice a pattern of errors, return to modeled instruction and reteach as necessary. It may be too early in the instructional cycle for the task, or the problem could be unclear directions. In either case, the role of the teacher is to ensure that students have the tools they need to engage with the task.

Conclusion

Our friend Jane is not only a brilliant teacher but also an astute observer of human nature.

It was Jane who introduced us to the notion of "cat people." Cat people are those of us who like our routines and generally stick to doing things the same way unless someone makes us, or convinces us, to do things differently. There's nothing wrong with being a cat person; in fact, most of us fall into this category, and most of our students do, too. The problem is, tendencies, habits, and comfort zones can sometimes get in the way of productive teaching and learning. Somewhere in our resistance to change lurks a fear.

Fear of failing is the elephant in teachers' classrooms—the question we secretly harbor but rarely utter aloud. Fear of our students' failure keeps us locked in the same practices that have become comfortable and familiar. It's also what keeps teachers in front of the classroom lecturing instead of turning learning over to the learners. We can speak of the student-centered classroom, but the worry that students lack the skills to pull it off can prevent teachers from taking those first steps toward productive group work.

But we know those steps are worth taking. We have explored together the many benefits of asking our students to engage each other in learning. They will learn more, feel better about themselves, and be more able to apply what they know if they learn cooperatively. We have discussed the right conditions teachers can create so that groups will be productive and become smarter than any of their individual members.

With an understanding of the principles of cooperative learning and practical routines for fostering them in group work, you are well equipped. You know to make the task challenging, which research shows actually increases a group's chance of success. You know to differentiate group work content, process, and products so that students with various readiness levels can all make unique contributions to a group. You have the models of our example teachers to help you as you teach skills and guide peer-to-peer interactions. You are ready to start on the road to developing cooperative and, ultimately, independent learners.

To support you along the way, we have included a list of questions to consider.* We hope these questions will help you plan and guide productive group work in your classroom.

Planning for Group Work

1. When you are planning your syllabus for the semester or year, how do you decide which topics, themes, or projects will lend themselves to group work?

2. How do you communicate or explain the objectives of the group task and define any relevant concepts to students (orally, in writing, by providing examples)?

3. How do you identify prerequisite skills students will need to successfully accomplish a specific project or task?

4. When and how do you teach students these skills?

Preparing Students to Work in Groups

1. Are there general skills students need to learn and practice in order to work productively in groups, regardless of the task or product (for example, active listening, helping one another master content, giving and receiving constructive criticism, and managing disagreements)?

2. How and when in the process do you teach them these skills?

---

*Adapted from *Tools for Teaching* (pp. 148–154) by Barbara Gross Davis. Copyright © 1993 by John Wiley & Sons, Inc. Reproduced with permission.

3. What are the biggest stumbling blocks for students getting started, and how do you help them overcome those obstacles?

4. Are there team-building exercises you do to help students when they are getting started?

Designing Group Work

1. How do you create tasks that require interdependence in which students are responsible to and dependent on others in the group?

2. How do you ensure that there is a fair division of labor for each member?

3. What kinds of rewards or encouragement do you use to support or motivate students working in groups?

4. How do you differentiate group tasks to ensure students are working at standard while accounting for differences in language and literacy skills?

5. How do students support peers in their group who struggle due to language or learning differences?

6. Do you ever use competitions or category winners?

7. Do students have opportunities to work together face to face as well as online?

Organizing Learning Groups

1. How do you organize students into groups? What do teachers with large numbers of English learners need to think about when organizing groups?

2. Is there an optimal size for groups?

3. How do you help groups to devise a plan of action (who will be doing what and when)?

4. How are decisions made within the group?

5. For tasks or projects that span a number of days or weeks, what processes do you use to check progress?

6. How do students deal with uncooperative members and manage conflicts?

Evaluating Group Work

1. How is group work evaluated (by the teacher, the group, and individuals)?

2. Does the evaluation include both the quality of the product and the effectiveness of the group?

3. How do you communicate the grading system to students?

4. Is there group work that is not formally evaluated? If yes, what feedback or assessments are used for this type of group work?

Dealing with Student Concerns About Group Work

1. How do you assess students' feeling about working in groups—particularly their prior experiences with group work and whether those experiences were positive or negative?

2. How do you deal with students who would rather work alone?

3. What happens when a group is not working out?

4. After working in groups, how do students' perceptions and feelings about group work change?

The Cooperative Road to Independent Learning

To close, we would like to step back from our focus on productive group work and look at it once again as part of the natural progression of gradually releasing responsibility to the learner. To be able to reflect on and assess their own learning, to plan next steps, to apply their learning in novel ways—these are the ultimate goals we hold for our students, which thoughtfully designed group work can move students toward. Through interactions with their teachers and peers, students come to a deeper understanding of themselves and the world around them. Neurobiologists have shown that the search for meaning is innate, and that meaning emanates from the learner, not the teacher (Diamond & Hopson, 1998). We want to give students the skills and confidence to make meaning themselves.

Dulce and Mario, two English language learners new to the country, showed us how successful this process can be. In their English language development class, a unit investigating immigration included studying *The Circuit: Stories from the Life of a Migrant Child* by Francisco Jiménez. Throughout the unit, students were read to by the teacher, read on their own, met with the teacher to discuss ideas, and worked in productive groups. They engaged in most of the instructional routines presented in this book—including quickwrites, graphic organizers, partner conversations, and peer response—in order to consolidate and expand their knowledge and ideas about immigration. Finally, at the end of the unit, the teacher asked students to complete an individual project: a poem about their own experience as an immigrant. Here are the poems Dulce and Mario wrote:

Dulce's Poem

How to say goodbye?
to the woman who gave me life,
to the family who grew me up,
to those who taught me never to give up . . .

How to say goodbye?
to all I know,
to all I used to do.

How hard to start a new life
in a new place
with new people

Moreover,
without my strongest support in life—
my mother

Saying goodbye
carries more than words alone;
the weight of grandparents and friends
are within me,
in deep solitude,
digging a hole in my life.

Mario's Poem

An August hot summer morning
I sat on the edge of my bed
wondering,

why am I leaving
my friends, my family,
the people who love me—
leaving my inspiration, my city, my country?

From my window
a wondrous sunrise,
the fresh sense of morning,
invaded my room
as I sat on the edge of my bed
wondering,
how to say goodbye
to the one who always listened,
who heard my first word
who was my first world?

A stream of tears fell
silently.
The hardest part began;
she knows I'm leaving, with
three minutes to tell her goodbye.
Enough time?
to say how much I love her

A river of tears fell
silently,
my voice of broken words
couldn't say goodbye.

Three minutes, a lifetime,
my heart beating
stopped feeling

How could I say goodbye?

The effect that the classroom environment and productive group work had on Dulce's and Mario's understanding of immigration is evident in these goodbye poems they wrote to their families. While most people who met these students during their first year of schooling in the United States might assume that they were struggling with school, their finished projects suggest a depth of understanding and skill that teachers everywhere hope for. Yes, they need to continue their development of academic English. But as you read the poems, picture for a moment these two young poets, standing in the presence of their teacher and peers, reading aloud their tributes to their families. They are not in this alone; they belong to a learning community. And yet they are also successful students, well on their way to becoming independent learners who can seek and make their own meaning. This is what we all want for them, and for all our students.

Resources

Allington, R. L. (2002, November). You can't learn much from books you can't read. *Educational Leadership, 60*(3), 16–19.

Alvermann, D. E., & Hagood, M. C. (2000, February). Fandom and critical media literacy. *Journal of Adolescent & Adult Literacy, 43*(5), 436–446.

Antil, L. R., Jenkins, J. R., Wayne, S. K., & Vadasy, P. F. (1998). Cooperative learning: Prevalence, conceptualizations, and the relation between research and practice. *American Educational Research Journal, 35*(3), 419–454.

Aronson, E. (2000). *Nobody left to hate: Teaching compassion after Columbine.* New York: W. H. Freeman.

Aronson, E., Blaney, N., Sikes, J., Stephan, C., & Snapp, M. (1978). *The jigsaw classroom.* Beverly Hills, CA: Sage.

Baron-Cohen, S., Leslie, A. M., & Frith, U. (1985). Does the autistic child have a "theory of mind"? *Cognition, 21*(1), 37–46.

Barron, B. J. S., Schwartz, D. L., Vye, N. J., Moore, A., Petrosino, A., Zech, L., & Bransford, J. D. (1998). Doing with understanding: Lessons from research on problem- and project-based learning. *Journal of the Learning Sciences, 7*(3–4), 271–311.

Battistich, V., Solomon, D., & Delucchi, K. (1993). Interactive processes and student outcomes in cooperative learning groups. *The Elementary School Journal, 94*(1), 19–32.

Bennett, N., & Cass, A. (1988). The effects of group composition on group interactive processes and pupil understanding. *British Educational Research Journal, 15*(1), 19–32.

Berk, L. E. N., & Winsler, A. (1995). *Scaffolding children's learning: Vygotsky and early childhood education.* Washington, DC: National Association for the Education of Young Children.

Billing, D. (2007, April). Teaching for transfer of core/key skills in higher education: Cognitive skills. *Higher Education, 53*(4), 483–516.

Bowen, C. W. (2000). A quantitative literature review of cooperative learning effects on high school and college chemistry achievement. *Journal of Chemical Education, 77*(1), 116–119.

Brookhart, S. M. (2008). *How to give effective feedback to your students.* Alexandria, VA: ASCD.

Cassady, J. K. (1998, Fall). Wordless books: No-risk tools for inclusive middle-grade classrooms. *Journal of Adolescent & Adult Literacy, 41*(6), 428–433.

Choudhury, S., Charman, T., & Blakemore, S. J. (2008, September). Development of the teenage brain. *Mind, Brain, & Education, 2*(3), 142–147.

Coates, G. (2005, September–October). Adventures in communication: Mathematics and English language development. *Connect, 19*(1), 11–13.

Cohen, E. G. (1994). *Designing groupwork: Strategies for the heterogeneous classroom.* New York: Teachers College Press.

Costa, A., & Kallick, B. (Eds.). (2000). *Habits of mind: A developmental series.* Alexandria, VA: ASCD.

Crain, W. C. (2005). *Theories of development: Concepts and application* (5th ed.). Upper Saddle River, NJ: Pearson/Prentice-Hall.

Davey, B. (1983). Think aloud—Modeling the cognitive processes of reading comprehension. *Journal of Reading, 27*(1), 44–47.

Davis, B. G. (1993). *Tools for teaching.* San Francisco: Jossey-Bass.

Decety, J., & Lamm, C. (2007, December). The role of the right temporoparietal junction in social interaction: How low-level computational processes contribute to meta-cognition. *The Neuroscientist, 13,* 580–593.

Decety, J., Michalska, K., & Akitsuki, Y. (2008, September). Who caused the pain? An fMRI investigation of empathy and intentionality in children. *Neuropsychologia, 46*(11), 2607–2614.

Diamond, M. N. C., & Hopson, J. (1998). *Magic trees of the mind: How to nurture your child's intelligence, creativity and healthy emotions from birth through adolescence.* New York: Dutton.

Doidge, N. (2007). *The brain that changes itself: Studies of personal triumph from the frontiers of brain science.* New York: Viking.

Duke, N. K., & Pearson, P. D. (2002). Effective practices for developing reading comprehension. In A. E. Farstup & S. J. Samuels (Eds.), *What research has to say about reading instruction* (pp. 205–242). Newark, DE: International Reading Association.

Fay, N., Garrod, S., & Carletta, J. (2000, November). Group discussion as interactive dialogue or as serial monologue: The influence of group size. *Psychological Science, 11*(6), 481–486.

Fisher, D., & Frey, N. (2001). *Responsive curriculum design in secondary schools: Meeting the diverse needs of students.* Lanham, MD: Scarecrow Education.

Fisher, D., & Frey, N. (2003, February). Writing instruction for struggling adolescent readers: A gradual release model. *Journal of Adolescent & Adult Literacy, 46*(5), 396–407.

Fisher, D., & Frey, N. (2007). *Checking for understanding: Formative assessment techniques for your classroom.* Alexandria, VA: ASCD.

Fisher, D., & Frey, N. (2008a). *Better learning through structured teaching: A framework for the gradual release of responsibility.* Alexandria, VA: ASCD.

Fisher, D., & Frey, N. (2008b). *Improving adolescent literacy: Content area strategies at work* (2nd ed.). Upper Saddle River, NJ: Pearson/Merrill/Prentice-Hall.

Flood, J., Lapp, D., Flood, S., & Nagel, G. (1992, April). Am I allowed to group? Using flexible patterns for effective instruction. *The Reading Teacher, 45*(8), 608–616.

Frey, N., & Fisher, D. (2005). *Language arts workshop: Purposeful reading and writing instruction.* Upper Saddle River, NJ: Pearson/Merrill/Prentice-Hall.

Giedd, J. N., Blumenthal, J., Jeffries, N. O., Castellanos, F. X., Liu, H., Zijdenbos, A., et al. (1999, October). Brain development during childhood and adolescence: A longitudinal MRI study. *Nature Neuroscience, 2*(10), 861–863.

Gilbert, S. J., & Burgess, P. W. (2008, September). Social and nonsocial functions of rostral prefrontal cortex: Implications for education. *Mind, Brain, & Education, 2*(3), 148–156.

Gillies, R. M. (2008). The effects of cooperative learning on junior high school students' behaviours, discourse, and learning during a science-based learning activity. *School Psychology International, 29*(3), 328–347.

Goodman, Y. (1985). Kidwatching: Observing children in the classroom. In A. Jaggar & M. T. Smith-Burke (Eds.), *Observing the language learner* (pp. 9–18). Newark, DE: International Reading Association.

Gorney, C. (2008, August 3). The urge to merge. *New York Times,* p. MM30. Retrieved April 2, 2009, from www.nytimes.com/2008/08/03/magazine/03traffic-t.html?ref=magazine

Graff, G., & Birkenstein, C. (2006). *"They say/I say": The moves that matter in academic writing.* New York: W. W. Norton & Company.

Hebb, D. O. (1949). *The organization of behavior: A neuropsychological theory.* New York: Wiley.

Hogan, K., Nastasi, B. K., & Pressley, M. (1999). Discourse patterns and collaborative scientific reasoning in peer and teacher-guided discussions. *Cognition & Instruction, 17*(4), 379–432.

House, J. D. (2005, September). Classroom instruction and science achievement in Japan, Hong Kong, and Chinese Taipei: Results from the TIMSS 1999 assessment. *International Journal of Instructional Media, 32*(3), 295–311.

Howard, P. J. (2006). *The owner's manual for the brain: Everyday applications from mind-brain research.* Austin, TX: Bard Press.

Hulse-Killacky, D., Killacky, J., & Donigian, J. (2001). *Making task groups work in your world.* Upper Saddle River, NJ: Merrill/Prentice-Hall.

Ives, B. (2007, May). Graphic organizers applied to secondary algebra instruction for students with learning disorders. *Learning Disabilities Research & Practice, 22*(2), 110–118.

Johnson, D. W., & Johnson, R. T. (1975). *Learning together and alone: Cooperative, competitive, and individualistic learning.* Englewood Cliffs, NJ: Prentice-Hall.

Johnson, D. W., & Johnson, R. T. (1994). *Leading the cooperative school* (2nd ed.). Edina, MN: Interaction Book Company.

Johnson, D. W., Johnson, R. T., & Holubec, E. J. (1998). *Circles of learning: Cooperation in the classroom* (7th ed.). Edina, MN: Interaction.

Kagan, S. (1994). *Cooperative learning.* San Clemente, CA: Resources for Teachers.

Kapur, M. (2008). Productive failure. *Cognition & Instruction, 26*(3), 379–424.

Lan, W. (2005, February). Self-monitoring and its relationship with educational level and task importance. *Educational Psychology, 25*(1), 109–127.

Law, Y. (2008, August). Effects of cooperative learning on second graders' learning from text. *Educational Psychology, 28*(5), 567–582.

LeDoux, J. E. (2002). *The synaptic self: How our brains become who we are.* New York: Viking.

Leonard, J. (2001). How group composition influenced the achievement of sixth-grade mathematics students. *Mathematical Thinking & Learning, 3*(2), 175–200.

Lieras, C. (2008, September). Do skills and behaviors in high school matter? The contribution of non-cognitive factors in explaining differences in educational attainment and earnings. *Social Science Research, 37*(3), 888–902.

McEwen, B. S. (2006). Protective and damaging effect of stress mediators: Central role of the brain. *Dialogues in Clinical Neuroscience, 8*(4), 283–297.

Meijnen, G. W., & Guldemond, H. (2002, September). Grouping in primary schools and reference processes. *Educational Research & Evaluation, 8*(3), 229–248.

Michaelsen, L., Fink, L. D., & Knight, A. (1997). Designing effective group activities: Lessons for classroom teaching and faculty development. In D. DeZure and M. Kaplan (Eds.), *To improve the academy* (pp. 373–397). Stillwater, OK: POD Network.

Montgomery, K. J., & Haxby, J. V. (2008, October). Mirror neuron system differentially activated by facial expressions and social hand gestures: A functional magnetic resonance imaging study. *Journal of Cognitive Neuroscience, 20*(10), 1866–1877.

Mueller, A., & Fleming, T. (2001). Cooperative learning: Listening to how children work at school. *The Journal of Educational Research, 94,* 259–265.

Oakes, J. (2005). *Keeping track: How schools structure inequality* (2nd ed.). New Haven, CT: Yale University Press.

Palincsar, A. S., Ransom, K., & Derber, S. (1988/1989, December/January). Collaborative research and development of reciprocal teaching. *Educational Leadership, 46*(4), 37–40.

Rizzolatti, G., & Craighero, L. (2004, July). The mirror-neuron system. *Annual Review of Neuroscience, 27,* 169–192.

Robinson, D. H. (1998, Winter). Graphic organizers as aids to text learning. *Reading Research & Instruction, 37*(2), 85–105.

Sansoti, F., & Powell-Smith, K. (2008, July). Using computer-presented social stories and video models to increase the social communication skills of children with high-functioning autism spectrum disorders. *Journal of Positive Behavior Interventions, 10,* 162–178.

Sapon-Shevin, M. (1998). *Because we can change the world: A practical guide to building cooperative, inclusive classroom communities.* Boston: Allyn and Bacon.

Shaaban, K. (2006, November–December). An initial study of the effects of cooperative learning on reading comprehension, vocabulary acquisition, and motivation to read. *Reading Psychology, 27*(5), 377–403.

Simmons, J. (2003, May). Responders are taught, not born. *Journal of Adolescent & Adult Literacy, 46*(8), 684–693.

Solomon, D., Watson, M., Battistich, V., Schaps, E., & Delucchi, K. (1996). Creating classrooms that students experience as communities. *American Journal of Community Psychology, 24,* 719–748.

Sommerville, J. A., & Decety, J. (2006). Weaving the fabric of social interaction: Articulating developmental psychology and cognitive neuroscience in the domain of motor cognition. *Psychonomic Bulletin & Review, 13*(2), 179–200.

Surowiecki, J. (2005). *The wisdom of crowds: Why the many are smarter than the few and how collective wisdom shapes business, economics, societies, and nations.* New York: Anchor Books.

Tate, M. L. (2003). *Worksheets don't grow dendrites: 20 instructional strategies that engage the brain.* Thousand Oaks, CA: Corwin.

Tomlinson, C. A. (1999). *The differentiated classroom.* Alexandria, VA: ASCD.

Tomlinson, C. A. (2001). *How to differentiate instruction in mixed-ability classrooms* (2nd ed.). Alexandria, VA: ASCD.

Tomlinson, C. A. (2003). *Fulfilling the promise of the differentiated classroom: Strategies and tools for responsive teaching.* Alexandria, VA: ASCD.

Tomlinson, C. A., Moon, T. R., & Callahan, C. M. (1997, Summer). Use of cooperative learning at the middle level: Insights from a national survey. *Research in Middle Level Education Quarterly, 20*(4), 37–55.

Towell, J. H. (1999/2000, December/January). Motivating students through music and literature. *The Reading Teacher, 53*(4), 284–287.

Vygotsky, L. S. (1978). *Mind in society: The development of higher psychological processes.* Cambridge, MA: Harvard University Press.

Webb, N. M., Nemer, K. M., & Ing, M. (2006). Small-group reflections: Parallels between teacher discourse and student behavior in peer-directed groups. *Journal of the Learning Sciences, 15*(1), 63–119.

West, K. R. (1998, April). Noticing and responding to learners: Literacy evaluation and instruction in the primary grades. *The Reading Teacher, 51*(7), 550–559.

Wright, J. K. (2005, November). "A discussion with myself on paper": Counseling and psychotherapy masters student perceptions of keeping a learning log. *Reflective Practice, 6*(4), 507–521.

Index

The letter *f* following a page number denotes a figure.

About the Authors

Nancy Frey, PhD, is a professor of literacy in the School of Teacher Education at San Diego State University and a classroom teacher at Health Sciences High & Middle College. Before joining the university faculty, Nancy was a special education teacher in the Broward County (Florida) Public Schools, where she taught students at the elementary and middle school levels. She later worked for the Florida Department of Education on a statewide project for supporting students with disabilities in a general education curriculum. Nancy is a recipient of the Christa McAuliffe Award for Excellence in Teacher Education from the American Association of State Colleges and Universities and of the Early Career Award from the National Reading Conference. Her research interests include reading and literacy, assessment, intervention, and curriculum design. She has published many articles and books on literacy and instruction, including *Reading for Information* and *Better Learning Through Structured Teaching* (both with Doug Fisher). She can be reached at nfrey@mail.sdsu.edu.

Douglas Fisher, PhD, is a professor of language and literacy education in the Department of Teacher Education at San Diego State University and a classroom teacher at Health Sciences High & Middle College. He is a member of the California Reading Hall of Fame and is the recipient of a Celebrate Literacy Award from the International Reading Association, the Farmer Award for Excellence in Writing from the National Council of Teachers of English, and a Christa McAuliffe Award for Excellence in Teacher Education from the American Association of State Colleges and Universities. He has published numerous articles on improving student achievement, and his books include *Creating Literacy-Rich Schools for Adolescents* (with Gay Ivey), *Checking for Understanding* (with Nancy Frey), and *Content-Area Conversations* (with Carol Rothenberg and Nancy Frey). He can be reached at dfisher@mail.sdsu.edu.

Sandi Everlove is the founder and chief academic officer at TeachFirst. She is the primary architect of a professional learning model that integrates online videos of research-based instructional practices, collaborative learning communities, leadership development, and onsite consulting. Prior to TeachFirst, Sandi was a high school chemistry teacher in Seattle Public Schools. She received the Washington State Golden Apple Award in 1998 and created an award-winning high school ethics course. A passionate advocate for children, she established and trained a mobile professional development team providing support for rural teachers in Guatemala and cofounded Lake Washington Girls Middle School, the first not-for-profit, secular all-girls middle school in Washington state. She can be reached at severlove@teachfirst.com.

Related ASCD Resources

At the time of publication, the following ASCD resources were available (ASCD stock numbers appear in parentheses). For up-to-date information about ASCD resources, go to www.ascd.org.

Mixed Media

Making School Improvement Happen with What Works in Schools: Teacher-Level Factors: An ASCD Action Tool by John L. Brown (#705054)

Teaching for Understanding: An ASCD Professional Inquiry Kit by Charlotte Danielson (#196212)

Print Products

The Art and Science of Teaching: A Comprehensive Framework for Effective Instruction by Robert J. Marzano (#107001)

Better Learning Through Structured Teaching by Douglas Fisher and Nancy Frey (#108010)

Classroom Instruction That Works: Research-Based Strategies for Improving Student Achievement by Robert J. Marzano, Deborah J. Pickering, and Jane E. Pollock (#10101)

Cooperative Learning in the Classroom by David Johnson, Edyth Holubec, and Roger Johnson (#194224)

Enhancing Professional Practice: A Framework for Teaching (2nd edition) by Charlotte Danielson (#106034)

Learning and Leading with Habits of Mind: 16 Essential Characteristics of Success edited by Arthur L. Costa and Bena Kallick (#108008)

Never Work Harder Than Your Students & Other Principles of Great Teaching by Robyn R. Jackson (#109001)

Video

The Art and Science of Teaching DVD Series (two 45-minute DVDs) (#608074)

Getting Results with Cooperative Learning (three 25- to 30-minute programs on one DVD with a Facilitator's Guide) (#605176)

A Visit to Classrooms of Effective Teachers (one 45-minute program with a comprehensive Viewer's Guide) (DVD: #605026; videotape: #405026)

For more information: send an e-mail to member@ascd.org; call 1-800-933-2723 or 703-578-9600 and press 2; send a fax to 703-575-5400; or write to Information Services, ASCD, 1703 N. Beauregard St., Alexandria, VA 22311-1714 USA.